VICTORIA FALLS
(ZAMBIA / ZIMBABWE BORDER, AFRICA)

One mile wide and 360 feet high!

2 ½ times higher than Niagara Falls and 3 times wider. Largest falls in the world when height and width are combined.

This is the Zambian side of the falls looking across towards the Zimbabwe side in the distance. I lived about 5 miles from there in the mid 1970's on this Zambian side in a city called Livingstone, named after David Livingstone who was the first European to see the falls. The locals call it the Mosi-oa-Tunya (The Smoke That Thunders)

Copyright © 2013 by Scott Hunter

God's Love Affair
by Scott Hunter

Printed in the United States of America

ISBN 9781626973510

All rights reserved solely by the author. The author guarantees all contents are original and do not infringe upon the legal rights of any other person or work. No part of this book may be reproduced in any form without the permission of the author. The views expressed in this book are not necessarily those of the publisher.

Unless otherwise indicated, Bible quotations are taken from the King James Version. Copyright © 1964 by Zondervan.

www.xulonpress.com

GOD'S LOVE AFFAIR

A Love Story Like None Other!

JOHN 3:16

"For God So Loved The World That He Gave His Only Begotten Son That Whosoever Believeth In Him Should Not Perish But Have Everlasting Life."

**Written By:
SCOTT HUNTER**

Now retired, but former missionary since 1972 with the Pentecostal Assemblies of Canada International Missions Department.

Would love to hear from my readers with comments on what has been written here. This one verse is a treasure house of inspiration and hope, which should cause all of us to rejoice greatly in His love for us and also in His Gift to us! To Him therefore be all the glory and praise!

Email me at: snhunter@gmail.com

D edicated to **Jonah and Matildah Kabwe**; great Zambia friends of mine ministering effectively for God in that African nation and region! Jonah conducts seminars throughout Zambia to train local church leadership there for the rapidly expanding national church nationwide!

They have been personal friends of ours for many years and greatly appreciated as such! We have traveled together both in Africa and also in Canada.

With close to two thousand national churches in the Pentecostal Assemblies of God Zambia with which he works, and I have also worked in the past, and that number still expanding rapidly, there is quite a challenge there to train local leadership for a variety of ministries within their own local churches. This is what the Kabwes are currently involved in there for that national church.

Jonas and Matildah Kabwe, Lusaka, Zambia

"On behalf of my wife Matilda and myself, we would like to express our thanks to God, and gratitude to Scott and Nancy Hunter for dedicating this awesome work of his life work on the Gospel of Christ to us. Matilda and I have known Scott and Nancy for over twenty-five years through his missionary work in Zambia. During all these years, he has been an inspiration to us in our ministry. This passionate and elaborate teaching on the grace of God through John 3:16, has been his favorite devotion and passion for life as long as we have known him.

My wife and I are so honored to be the ones to whom this book is dedicated, considering the facts of his ministry experiences, includes the loss of his precious son Darryn Hunter, who went to be with the Lord in 1988. He would have been the most appropriate beneficiary. This proves Scott's unfailing love towards Matilda and I, for which we are so grateful. May this book find its way to men and women whose love for souls inspires them to levels of commitment and sacrifice far above and beyond the call of duty."

Jonah and Matilda Kabwe
PAOGz Zambia.

ACKNOWLEDGMENT: To two great friends, **Cindy McDonald** and **Melva Tulk**, for their much appreciated proofreading and editing of the script of this book! So love and appreciate both of you so much.

With special thanks as well to my wife, **Nancy Hunter**, for her computer expertise!

Scott Hunter Contact: snhunter@gmail.com

Table of Contents

CHAPTER		INDEX
Chapter 1	For God	Certainty 15
Chapter 2		Omnipotence . 23
Chapter 3		Process 31
Chapter 4	So Loved	Sovereignty . . 38
Chapter 5		Spontaneous. . 49
Chapter 6		Immeasurable. . 55
Chapter 7		Passion. 62
Chapter 8		Eternal 71
Chapter 9	The World	Range 76
Chapter 10	That He Gave	Action 91
Chapter 11	His Only Begotten Son	
		Gift 109
Chapter 12	That Whosoever	Scope. 126
Chapter 13	Believeth In Him	Message . . . 131
Chapter 14	Should Not Perish	Protection . . 142
Chapter 15	But Have Everlasting Life	Results 150

SECTION TWO

This second section of the book deals with the same verse, but is written from a world missions perspective instead!

Introduction to World Missions Section 163

1	For God	Source	 169
2	So Loved	Motivation	. . 174
3	The World	Objective	. . . 180
4	That He Gave	Action	 184
5	His Only Begotten Son		
		Solution	 190
6	That Whosoever	Range	 194
7	Believeth In Him	Proclamation	. 197
8	Should Not Perish	Security	 202
9	But Have Everlasting Life	Outcome	. . . 205

Introduction

This verse in John 3:16 is likely the best known verse in the whole of Scripture, and to anyone who reads it carefully it is quite obvious as to why it most certainly is just that. The verse takes us from God in the beginning, before we were ever created in Eden, to the eternities future where we will be forever with Him, and that is an extremely exciting journey for us to be taking.

I have loved this passage all my life, and have preached many times myself on every part of this one particular verse. I personally spent years as a missionary in Zambia, South Africa and also Malawi, and I still hear from many of my African friends via facebook from these countries, telling me they remember my speaking on this verse. One of them even told me he has tried a number of times to "repeat" my sermons on that verse and wanted my notes. Well here are some of them!

God "so loved" and redeemed us so that we could also "so love" Him, and then share His love with our world. Some wonderful day in eternity we will all join hands, and then shout for joy at that very process that made heaven possible for all of us who are there. So enjoy your reading of my thoughts on God's love affair with our world!

Blessings!

Scott Hunter (Former missionary to Africa; now retired) snhunter@gmail.com

CHAPTER 1

"FOR GOD" THE CERTAINTY OF HIS LOVE

The creation of our whole universe began with, "In the beginning God…." (Genesis 1:1) What a masterpiece He did produce in just a few short days, with the whole creation process culminating with Adam and Eve as His ultimate creation in the Garden of Eden. Actually, the fact it was all such a total masterpiece should certainly not be any surprise to anyone, for anything that begins with God is sure to be amazing at the very least. What else would we expect from the Almighty when He sets about to create?

Unfortunately Satan interfered badly in that wonderful original creation, and in the process caused Adam and Eve to severely mess up in that beautiful garden. He consequently led them in an open rebellion against God. It was at Satan's own personal, specific invitation for them to do so that had caused them to join him in that rebellion as well.

Regrettably things radically changed negatively for our whole human race from that point forward. Both time and eternity were consequently dramatically affected for us as a result of that Satan-inspired rebellion in Eden, which had dragged our first parents away from serving God as they were originally created to do so, and from there into an open rebellion against God instead.

John 3:16 is consequently a condensing of God's response to Eden's rebellion against Him. Satan certainly had no idea at the time of his move towards Eve, of the extent to which God would eventually go to reverse these adverse eternal results of that rebellion he was leading there in Eden that day.

But John takes the time here to really simplify, in just this one verse, the whole process of what God actually did do in order to reestablish that severed relationship between us and Him. In doing so he shows us the plan, protection, process, and Person that God used to negate these potential negatives of that original rebellion for anyone who would wish to be set free from them, and also from their dreadful eternal consequences.

I for one am so very grateful this verse begins as it does for us, and that it actually does not start instead with something such as; "As a result of that rebellion God…." If His action presented in this verse had been based upon what that rebellion actually deserved, it would have been a very sad day indeed, and in actual fact, leading to a sad eternity as well for all of us.

Or suppose the word "for" was simply an "if" instead? "If God so loved the world He would have……" That would also have been quite serious for us, because then there would be nothing we could be certain of until we knew for sure if He actually did do anything positive for us. But the use of the word "for" here to introduce this verse states a definite, indisputable reality; He simply does; it is a certainty. There is nothing to prove in relationship to that certain reality. He just does love us! That is certainly such a positive way to start. It is not "if God", but is instead; "for God"! There are no questions here whatsoever; simply total confidence in an emphatically stated realty.

Therefore it is so very fortunate that the verse actually does start with "for God", and that it does not in any way zero in on that rebellion in Eden whatsoever, nor any later private, personal sins of any of Adam's descendants which followed. Instead it focuses our attention in a completely different direction, with one hundred percent positive results fully guaranteed to anyone interested. Nothing is forced upon anyone, but actually instead of any kind of force, an open invitation for forgiveness is offered to anyone who would ever wish to accept that offer. And why would anyone ever not want to reach out and freely accept such a free gift?

"For" sets the stage to explain His reason behind the whole process that follows it. But when "God" is added to the word "for", the concept really begins to get quite interesting. For here is the One who has both the capacity, and also the total right to do anything He so pleases, now stepping into our situation.

He made it all, and that includes all of us as well, so why should He not then have every right, as well as the complete capacity, to do just as He pleases with, to or for us? As a result of His ability to do so, and also His certain right to act as He so desires, when we then read "For God", we could easily be wondering what would be coming next if we did not already know the end of this great story already.

I have a feeling I would personally be very nervous indeed about reading any further if I did not already know that final outcome, and in fact, already have begun to experience it personally in my own life. He could so easily have pronounced judgement on all of us, and then proceeded to start all over again with a completely new try.

But fortunately for us He did not go in that direction whatsoever. It was certainly a new beginning for sure, but that new beginning did not involve wiping out His "first try", and then starting anew a second time. Instead He lovingly made a "second chance" option available to His "first try" from Eden. We can be reborn, and begin anew at that transition point. The past becomes a buried past, and the future turns into a bright one for anyone who accepts the provision from this loving move of the Creator towards us.

In fact, the move was so far to the positive extreme that it is almost too good to be true, but it certainly is true nevertheless. This is actually not one of these situations where we could say that if it sounds too good to be true, then it likely is just that; not true! But this one is certainly the exception to that statement; it is too good to be true, but it is still true nevertheless!

For God started it all, and then invited us to participate in the solution at our own freewill, and thereby in so doing, take full advantage of every single aspect of all of the benefits offered. That is the God we serve; one with the power and also the right to take any action against rebellion He wished to take, yet the only action he did take was an extremely positive move towards us based solely upon His great love He certainly had to show and also express for us.

As a result, this whole process in the redemption of His fallen creation begins with "For God". The original creation was for God's pleasure, but when that relationship was severed by our willful sin, God certainly did not receive any pleasure from us from that point onward, so the relationship simply had to be fully restored.

No wonder we are told Jesus set His face with great determination towards Jerusalem that day, despite His knowing in advance what was awaiting Him there on Calvary! He wanted that relationship fully restored as soon as possible, and nothing was ever going to distract Him from seeing the process for this reunion fully accomplished and put into operation. So with great resolve and determination He headed towards that city and that cross He knew was awaiting Him there.

For that very reason, the reestablishing of the relationship to a two-way love affair between God and His prize creation was initiated by God, because it surely was His top priority in all of creation to have us close to Him forever anyway. Nothing else mattered to Him anything close to that one primary objective; He simply had to get us back to Himself once again!

It is certainly an understatement to say that doing so was even His number one priority. Actually it was really His only priority! This is a certainty beyond dispute. This love affair began with Him, so He naturally became the "aggressor" to see it become a two-way love affair once more, and He had no other objective, even from the far reaches of eternity past, other than to ensure it was fully restored no matter what the personal cost to Him might actually be, and He certainly already knew that total cost to Himself even at that time.

"For God" reached out to us in love, and for the joy of our returning that love to Him in the future, He "endured the cross and despised the shame" to give us a second chance to do so. Once God stepped in and got personally involved, then anything was possible, and certainly what did happen from there onward was surely eternity changing for us.

We therefore need to daily thank Him for doing just that in such a wonderful, positive way. Eternity would have been so very dark for us indeed had He not chosen to do what He did, but we do not now even need to consider that terrible possibility any more, for He certainly did get involved, and that action potentially changed everything for us eternally.

At Calvary, He there reached out to us collectively, but He also now reaches out to us individually as well. Now we must personally be certain to respond to His outreached hand to us, because it is backed by His loving heart for us. So do not count yourself out, or exclude yourself because you ignored its generous provision. It is far too good to resist or to just ignore.

A multi millionaire offers someone a large stack of cash, but instead of accepting it, they simply shake their heads, say "No thanks", and then simply walk casually away from him. Who would ever be crazy enough to do such a thing? The offer is certain and so easily accessible. All that needs to be done is to take the offer seriously, and then simply accept it from Him.

This verse actually explains it so very simply for us that even a child can so easily understand its life-changing message. For God, and then everything that follows that introduction shows us His positive move towards us, and also the wonderful consequences of that move if we simply accept Him and His covering. He provided the solution, and we simply only have to accept that provision that is now there for us. There certainly is nothing too profound or too complicated about the process.

As we look at that verse, one of the first and most interesting realities that stands out to us is the total lack of any mention by God of our transgressions, or any other condemning negatives about us here focused upon whatsoever.

That amazing fact certainly does not mean there were none, nor does it mean in any way that God was unaware of any that did exist. As well, it certainly does not mean that any which did exist were of no great concern for God Himself either. God knew all the details, but He still chose to approach us from a totally different perspective completely.

No negatives were involved in His approach to us. It was totally positive towards us all the way both in motivation and also in outcome. In fact, God's actual stated need to originally take action on our behalf implies that He was very much aware of all of the negatives. But instead of referring to them, He simply chooses to tell us about His love-inspired solution, rather than remind us again of our rebellion!

This silence on His part regarding our rebellion and sin does not in any way minimize the seriousness of the sin. Instead it serves as a wonderful indication and reminder of His complete forgiveness of them all as a result of that very intense love which He surely has for us all.

CHAPTER 2

"For God"
The Omnipotence
of His Love

So we begin with "for God", and it is because of the "for God" that the whole of the remainder of this verse actually did happen. In reality, what could have followed that "for God" had the potential to actually be quite radical in either a negative or a positive way for all of us!

The offended Creator of everything is now responding to that rebellion against Himself in the Garden of Eden, and against His right to be King and ruler over His own creation. God is about to intervene in our affairs because of that rebellion, and that fact should get our attention immediately, and should certainly easily hold it for quite a while.

We rightfully could seriously wonder at this point if that rebellion against Him there actually did have any negative effects upon His personal feelings towards us. If so, how is He then going to act to "get even" or to "settle the score" with us for that open rebellion? Since God is about to react to our rebellion against Him by our original parents in Eden, it could be quite serious for all of us for now and certainly for eternity.

On that basis, two questions readily come to mind immediately; firstly for what reason is He going to take this action; is it a positive or negative reason, and secondly in what way is He going to react to our actual open treason. Will it be an extremely good move towards us, or otherwise perhaps be an action that could have terrible consequences for all of us for eternity?

"For God" and you just cannot get any better Mover than that for sure. If you have a problem, and there is no doubt we certainly all did inherit a major one because of Eden, then there is surely no better "intervener" to help with that situation than to have God Himself step into it. I will willingly step aside at any time to allow Him into any situation in my own personal life. And the solving of the problem associated with our original rebellion is certainly one I absolutely trust Him with, especially since I have come to know Him in the way I now do.

So we gladly tell Him, "God, You are most welcome. In fact, You are most desperately needed, in our lives now and forever, for where would we actually be today without You?" It is no wonder we sing so passionately "How Great Thou Art"! So we can now confidently step aside, and let Him get totally involved, for when it starts with "For God" we can certainly trust in whatever will then follow that introduction for this verse!

"Therefore we sincerely thank you, God, for that marvelous intervention, and for Your personally getting involved with us; especially for what You then set about to do for our whole lost race once You did get into the process of "fixing" that problem that Satan introduced us to that tragic day. It sure has worked miracles in Your doing just that for us, Lord."

"I know there is absolutely nothing I can do that will come close to repaying You, Lord, for doing so, nor am I ever capable of loving you enough to express my gratitude, but I do promise I will spend my whole life trying to do so, and then when You increase my capacity to love in heaven, I will continue to do so there with all that increased capacity to love as well!"

For God made the first move, and that first move certainly was as far from a negative move towards us as it was possible for it to be. Negatives were not any part of His thinking, nor in any way involved in the motivation for His action He undertook for us either. Instead it was a one hundred percent positive reaction on God's part to a one hundred percent original rejection situation from us at the beginning of our history; a totally positive reaction to our negative rejection of Him.

Here in this situation God is certainly seen as the "aggressor" because we were obviously totally helpless ourselves in our situation, but thankfully He was a totally loving aggressor towards us in His actions. That fact is not even debatable. He made the first move, and it was certainly an extremely aggressive one at that, in righting the wrong and potentially fixing the whole problem for us if we simply accept the solution He provided.

I personally am so thankful for such an aggressive God who just does not "sit on the sidelines" and judges. He is "right in the game" Himself with us, and certainly not just one of those "experts" who simply sits in the stands and passes his negative comments on the players on the field, but yet does not have what it takes to be on the field himself. But our God was never on the sidelines; He was in the game with us right from the very start.

His approach certainly was not passive in any way or form. Instead it was a move in response to an "outside influence" on Him; and that "outside influence" was the heartbreaking separation from Him of the object of His passionate love. He simply had to have us back!

I love such an aggressive God in a situation like this; a God who makes the first move towards us without waiting for someone else to make the initial move toward Him. So He certainly made that first move Himself, and now He simply responds both in and also with total, immediate love to any move that is ever made towards Him by us to take advantage of His first move towards us.

But waiting for any first positive move from us towards Him was surely not God's way of operating in His loving relationship he had with us. In fact, He was certainly the one who "asked for the first date". The love affairs started with Him, and I am certainly one of the many millions who are so very happy to have then responded to Him, and also to His amazing love that still even now flows out so freely and so abundantly to all of us.

This loving relationship from God to us started from the eons of the ages past before the worlds were even formed and will still flow out to us into the yet eternal future, and that certainly is the very best example that I know of for a long-term relationship of love. It started with God and since God is both eternal as well as unchanging, it is a totally secure relationship between Himself as the Giver and us as its object. Now we return it to Him as well, and begin a two-way relationship of love that will continue into eternity.

In Eden it tragically became totally a one-sided love relationship. Instead of the joy of a two-way loving relationship it became nothing but heartache and heartbreak for the Creator from there onward until that relationship was finally totally restored once again once we accepted His full pardon for ourselves.

Interestingly, when we look at that reconciliation process we have a tendency to think mostly of what Jesus did for us, and the personal benefits it therefore brought to us, and for certain that was one supreme act of love for us that He actually did demonstrate on Calvary. For Him to so willingly go from the throne room of the universe to being nailed almost naked to a cross was quite a demonstration of His love without any doubt. It was certainly quite a wonderful move for Him to make for us, but also especially a move towards us to get us fully back into His family.

But we must also never forget this other awe inspiring fact as well; that the Father is also very much involved in that act of love towards us right along with His Son as well. The Father also actually loved us so much that He had to give us His Son, and I suspect His "giving" of His Son that day was as difficult for the Father as the "going" was for His Son!

So we must remember that Calvary also cost the Father very dearly as well. It was not an easy, casual decision for Him to decide to give such a precious Gift as His only Son to such an extreme degree of giving because of His actual love for us, for we need to remember He also dearly loved His Only Begotten Son passionately as well.

Children sing, "Jesus loves me this I know..." and that fact is surely such a wonderful reality to their young lives; to know that they are actually loved by Jesus. What a joy to be loved, but what a great joy it is for them to also know they are actually loved by Jesus, but that is certainly not the whole story. This love affair for us is far greater even than that, and for that reality we will continually be so eternally thankful.

The love process started with the whole Godhead loving us; God, and that is the total Trinity; Father, Son and Holy Spirit. Therefore we can now easily add two more verses to that kids' song; one about the Father also loving, and yet another about the Holy Spirit loving them as well. "The Father loves me this I know for the Bible also tells me so."

This was certainly not any frivolous love affair for us by the Son that the Father was actually trying to discourage because the cost to both all of them would be too high to face. It was equally passionate toward us from all three members of the loving Triune God. It is a "Family" love affair with us!

It is fairly obvious to anyone looking closely at this whole affair that Satan's primary objective in the whole Eden scenario was to bring as much grief and heartache to God as he could possibly do so. So Satan targeted the primary object of God's love to break the relationship between us. He did not want us to give God the love that God so desperately needed from us, so he went after our first parents to stop it from ever happening.

And I do have to admit here that he certainly did succeed on that one, but fortunately only for a period of time. Then God aggressively stepped into the situation with a major solution to the problem Satan had created, and that solution certainly proved to us beyond any doubt just how much He actually did love us. The extremity, cost and total scope of the solution He provided showed us that God's love was far more than just easy talk on His part. This love was for real!

Satan's negative action towards us therefore turned instead into a major setback for Satan himself, for it made our response to God's love for us more passionate than it could ever have been had that original interference by Satan not taken place. Therefore we love Him now as both our Creator and as our Sovereign King, but we also now love Him because he became our Rescuer and Redeemer as well. Satan worse action towards us turned into another great incentive for us to love God even more that ever!

"So I guess you lost that one badly, Satan, despite what you did cost God to "fix" the problem you caused. As a consequence of what you did to us, Satan, and also as a result of God's response to it, we have a far greater motivation to love God than we could ever have had if this had not happen in the beginning." (And I certainly hope you read this paragraph personally, Satan!!)

Now we know that God is not only our Creator and our King; but we also now know Him as our Lover and as our Redeemer, and these latter two are a direct result of Satan's action against us, and then of God's solution to that very action of Satan himself.

"For God" and then nothing else matters, for God plus nothing else whatsoever equals one hundred percent total! When our loving God entered the picture, we were then totally safe. John certainly should now have gotten our full attention as soon as he penned, "For God". I just cannot wait to see what will follow next, now that God has been introduced here as having gotten personally involved in our situation.

When we consider this redemption process, we usually look upon the whole procedure from the perspective of God intervening in our desperately needy situation to do His best to bring help to us in our dire need. And it certainly is that without any doubt.

But John here adds another perspective to this whole redemption process, for he makes it clear that God Himself also had a serious "problem" which needed to be dealt with here as well. Talking about God having any kind of need or problem may sound rather strange at first, but He actually did have a very serious need indeed, and we will talk about that fact in the next chapter.

CHAPTER 3

"For God" The Process of God's Love

So the salvation story so fantastically condensed and then presented here in this verse begins with God's personal need being met for Him as well, as He so lovingly sets about the process of meeting our needs for us. God really did need us back to Himself. That is the whole story behind redemption, and what a wonderful story it actually is for certain!

It is clear that salvation came to us because God Himself loved us, and He needed us back in a loving, close relationship with Himself, after Satan had broken that relationship with his sin, and his then causing our original parents (Adam and Eve) to also sin by rebelling against His authority. (See Genesis 3:1-10 for the accounting of that tragic event in Eden)

Salvation is therefore also about meeting God's own personal need to be able to fully love us, and have our love expressed back to Him in return in order that He could Himself revel in it for eternity. The problem, as already stated, was that it was previously only a one-sided love affair, and God desperately needed for it to become a two-way passion.

Calvary was therefore designed to fix that total problem for us forever, and meet the need from both directions; our need for eternal help and security, and also God's need for our love to be fully focused upon Him forever as well. It certainly did accomplish both!

We were not created to be mere "monkeys" for God to play with occasionally, but instead to be His children; to be passionately loved forever by Himself, and for us to love Him in return as well. I fully realize God's capacity to love us far outreaches our ability to return that love to Him at present, but I have high expectations that God will immensely increase our capacity to love when we meet Him face to face some day.

I certainly expect I will be given a much greater capacity to love Him then, and maybe even a greater capacity to love all of you as well that day. I just cannot wait to see you all there in heaven some day, so I can try out that latter one myself on all of you, so be sure to join me there!

I have an adopted sister. Her mother died when she was about two years old and my parents adopted her just before her mother died. I was about ten years old at the time. It was great suddenly having a baby sister in the family!

Actually adoptions are quite interesting, and are usually motivated from three different and quite distinct directions. Firstly, there is the child's obvious need for a secure home, love, security, provision and many other such needs. That one is quite obvious.

But there are two other motivations behind adoptions as well. First, there is the need of the adopting parents to have someone to call their own; to shower their love and attention upon. That is certainly a very real factor in adoptions, but there is also another motivation, and that third one is the parent's need to have the child's love and attention directed back towards them as well. The parents need the love of the child for themselves. It is both great to love and also to be loved back in return as well.

That is what makes adoptions so wonderful. It establishes and legitimizes a two-way love affair that meets both participants love need from both directions; the need to be loved and the need to have someone to love in return as well! That is why God made the first move towards us that He has become so "famous" for having made that day; to meet this two-directional need of a loving relationship for both us and also for God Himself as well.

Can you see these three motives in John 3:16; our obvious need for a loving Father, but the Father's need for "children" to personally love Himself, and also then to receive their love in return back to Him? These are quite powerful motivations, meeting needs in both the giver and also in the receiver as well. He has so wonderfully met my need to be loved that I delight in returning that love to Him, and then sharing it with the world. In fact, that was His plan from the very start.

That is why the greatest and yet the simplest recounting of the plan of the redemptive potential for humanity begins with the two words "For God. . . .." We were drowning, but the help did not come to us because of our calling out for assistance. There was no SOS call from us. We were simply drowning and didn't even realize that terrifying fact.

Instead the call came to us from Him, because the Rescuer loved the drowning victim so intently He felt He had no other choice but to "jump into the raging water" to rescue us despite its "endangering" His life! That is the most natural reaction for anyone motivated by love for the victim; get into the water somehow no matter what the personal danger may obviously be! The victim has to be reached and rescued no matter what the cost.

What an amazing reality it is that He made that first move; stepping from heaven into the filthy society of the Roman controlled Middle East and "dropping" His Son as a mere baby right into the midst of it all. For God could not wait any longer to get us back into His arms, so the filth, poverty, occupation by a foreign, atheistic power, corruption, sin, greed, and the religious hypocrisy of that day did not deter Him in any way whatsoever. It was time for Him to step into the mess Himself and He certainly aggressively did just that beyond doubt!

The tree He had planted to form the cross for His Son to later die upon was already beginning to grow on a hillside near Jerusalem. So it was time for Him to begin the process which would restore His original intent in Eden; to love and also be loved in return, with no barriers whatsoever between Him and us to interfere in any way with that love relationship between us.

So God sent the archangel Gabriel to Israel to have a "chat" with a young virgin named Mary. In Luke 1:26-38 we have the record of that world-changing encounter between the two of them recorded for us. Just the mere meeting itself must have been quite a startling experience for Mary, but the message Gabriel delivered to her that day; can you just imagine her shock there at that time?

"Mary, you are going to have a son, whom you will call Jesus. He will be called the Son of the Most High" (vs 31, 32) "Me; but how is that possible? What will people say? What will Joseph think? I could be killed for this for I am not even married yet! How can I have a child since I am still a virgin? Are you really sure that God has actually chosen me to give birth to our long promised Messiah?"

You can just imagine her questions that day. Some of them are recorded in that chapter in Luke, but I strongly suspect she had a whole lot more questions for the angel than what are recorded here for us! Would not any young unmarried lady respond the same if she were the one Gabriel was talking to at that time and bringing her that startling message! But the angel simply says to her, "Yes, Mary, you are the chosen vessel! Your Child will be the Son of the most high! For God is stepping into His creation to bring help, and you, Mary, will be the channel to bring that promise to an actual reality!"

Have you ever wondered how that young unmarried woman felt about that news from Gabriel that day, and about the crucial part she would play in its fulfillment? Yet despite any possible negative consequence for her, and also the years of personal attention God's Son would certainly require from her, she nevertheless readily agreed to the challenge and responsibility by simply saying to Gabriel, "be it unto me according to your word!" Now there is trust for certain!

"Thank you, Mary, for agreeing to be the one to bring my Redeemer into the world, and then so lovingly and carefully raising Him in your humble home, so that He would later be able to die as the Sacrifice for my sins on Calvary."

"For God!"; and we stand back in awe at the fact this verse, which so concisely and accurately presents the total concept of salvation, begins with the offended God Himself making the first reconciliation move towards the offenders, and not the offenders having to first come to beg for His forgiveness instead. Not only did He make the first move in the reconciliation process, but it was a move that was so amazingly positive that the world has celebrated it every year since then for over two thousand years to date.

Our loving God made that first move towards us, and that fact makes Him stand out even today. The Scriptures tell us that our God actually "became sin for us" when He took the whole load of our guilt upon Himself, and He willingly bore the punishment for all of them Himself. It was Jehovah, God, and certainly not any other deity, who made that loving move towards our very lost world. Therefore He is the only One who deserves our worship and our love.

This brings a two-fold motivation to the church's challenge for reaching the world with that message of what God did! Even though we certainly recognize and acknowledge that human need is a great motivation for missions, yet it is God's need for love from us and from our world that is the greater motivation for our now reaching out to our world with the wonderful, life-giving message of what He did for us that day on Calvary.

"For God" The Process of God's Love

This fact brings another sobering reality to our response to God's Great Commission to us individually, and also to the church as a whole. Do we love God enough to dedicate our lives to fulfilling this passionate need so real to Him? He needs the world's love for eternity, and He went to quite an extreme to make that possible! The question then arises as to how far we are willing to go to ensure He receives their love also which He so richly deserves.

So now we need to move into our world to make it known to them! He will certainly show His appreciation for our doing so when you see Him face to face. He actually took it seriously enough, but do we also now look upon God's need for the world's love for Himself seriously as well?

I am so glad it was God who stepped into our situation and not someone else who merely "interfered". Satan had "stuck his nose into our affairs", and in doing so caused such a terrible problem for us, but he was totally beaten in his own game by God's actions and therefore our love, appreciation and affection now instead go totally to our loving God.

So it all begins with God; but what was God's motivation; what did God then do as a result of this motivation, and what action did God then take in relationship to it? Read on; for it is so very exciting to see just what God's motivation was and what He actually did do for us as a result of it! It has to do totally with His intense passion which comes next.

CHAPTER 4

"So Loved"
The Sovereignty
of His Love

❦

"God so ….", and it is here this verse could really begin to make us nervous. He "so" something, but then what happened? He so hated, so despised or any such word could have followed this word "so", especially when our rebellion against Him is considered. He is the sovereign God, and therefore had every right to make any decision He desired to make in relationship to our rebellion against Him. He is sovereign, so why should He not have such a right?

"So" is such a tiny word, yet we often use it to emphasize extremes. We make such statements as "it is so cold", "I am so sick", or "you are so beautiful". But when we place that word "so" after the word "God", who is the sovereign, almighty power of the universe, but also before His motivation for some action He is about to undertake relating to us, we have to seriously wonder just what that motivation is going to be, and certainly question how His response to that motivation will affect us. Will it be a negative or will it be a positive response to us?

We also fully realize that God's motivation for that action which He took is to such an extreme John needed to use that word "so" here to introduce it. In fact, there was likely no better word that John could have used to describe His actual motivation for this specific action. Therefore we surely have to wonder just what will come next. Whatever that motivation and whatever the resulting action, both are going to be very radical and dramatically affect us for certain.

God and "so" placed together in that way certainly have unlimited possibilities in consequences for us because of our sin and rebellion against Him. So what does God "so" do? We will have a look at His motivation firstly, and then later examine the actual action which He did take based upon that specific motivation that prompted it.

Here then is that motivation that was and continues to be behind it all; "God so loved"; past, present and future tense! God so loved us all that He actually did "so love" us, and that is not a miswritten sentence here by any means. He so loved us collectively but He also so loved us individually as well. It is a totally, one hundred percent active love, with nothing passive in it in any way whatsoever. He just loved to the extreme, and we certainly recognize that "so" is such a limited word to use here to describe that so unlimited love, but what else can be used to describe His love anyway?

We may very well wonder if such a thing is actually possible. We shook our fists in His face from Eden forward, and yet He still so loved us despite that rebellious action. Such a love is certainly amazing, to say the very least. In the beginning God created us, but also in the very beginning God also loved us. To love us was a sovereign act of His own will, and absolutely nothing could in any way change that reality.

Actually He loved us even before He created us, so loving us was not an afterthought on God's part. It was not a "they are so cute" thought by God after He created us, then saw His creation face to face, and as a result He there decided to love us. It was the actual reason He created us anyway; that we could become the object of His great love, and for Him to then be also loved in return by us for what He had so willingly done for us. God simply wanted a personal lover all for Himself, and He created us specifically for that very reason!

Crudely put, His loving us before creation was like parents loving their yet unconceived child, but that loving continued even after the rebellion our original parents became personally involved in against their very Creator in Eden. Yet God still loved us even then, and could not simply stand back and allow us to get totally away from Him, and then separated from His love forever. He had to have us back totally for Himself, no matter what the cost might be to Him.

Imagine parents passionately loving a very rebellious child. We easily recognize that the child certainly does not deserve their love because of the child himself in any way actually loving his parents, because he simply does not love them. In fact, everything that the child does only serves to contribute even more towards making that love towards him by the parents even less deserved.

At the same time, it also greatly increases the heartache of the loving parents because of that continued rebellion.

Yet the parents continues to love the wayward child no matter what that child may continue to do, and also continues to do everything possible to let that rebellious child know he is so very much loved, and still so very welcome back home at any time he wishes to return, with no questions asked whatsoever. It is the parent's decision to love the child no matter what the child may do. It is certainly not the child's decision whatsoever as to whether the parents can love him or not. And so it is with God's love for us; it is totally His own sovereign decision! Nobody can dispute that reality; it is His decision alone, and so He just loves us.

That is God! He knew us and He also knew our rebellion, yet He loved us so intentionally and did so despite all of these negatives. It is such an amazing love for certain! It is no wonder we glory in His embrace when we finally make our way back home to Him and find Him waiting there patiently for us to return to Him. The love of God truly is greater far than any tongue or pen could ever tell. Of that fact there surely is no doubt.

Now we are faced with the task of trying to explain the unexplainable of how He could so love us despite our failings, and then also try to help others to fathom that unfathomable love He has for them as well in their own personal situation. We try to understand; we let our minds run to the extreme limit of our capacity to grasp this truth, but we find we are no nearer the full understanding of its reality than we were when we started. That impossibility is surely easy enough for us to grasp when we realize we are actually trying to understand both love and God in a single context.

How is it humanly possible to grasp an unlimited love of an unlimited God with our very limited human capacity to understand? The King of glory actually does love us. It is His own decision, and since He is the sovereign King, He has every right to do so. Nobody tells the King He cannot do as He so wishes to do. He is the only One who makes all such decisions for Himself, for He is truly the only sovereign decision maker.

So His love for us is certainly a sovereign love for sure. Nobody ever told God to love us, and nobody can ever tell Him that he cannot love us either. That is His choice, and it is His choice alone. His love is "sovereign" simply because He is also sovereign Himself.

Bow your head before Him and worship Him and He will certainly love you. That fact is not likely too difficult to understand. But totally reject His love, and even deny His very existence, or actually curse Him shamelessly to the heavens, and He will just as certainly still continue to love you. To love us in that way is a sovereign decision of a sovereign God, and who can dispute the Creator's right to do so?

Sorry; but no matter what you may do, you simply cannot get beyond the reach of His love. That fact is final! Actually I am not really sorry at all for that amazing reality. Instead I am extremely delighted His love for any and all of us is so beyond anyone's personal decision except His very own, and that we cannot exempt ourselves from it here no matter what we do or even think. He is the total "Boss" here on this one, and not one of us has any choice in this matter here. He is going to love us anyway no matter what, so we may as well accept that fact right from the start and revel in its certainty.

So God's love for the world was and continues to be just such an amazing sovereign love, for it is quite simply a divine act by a sovereign God. "So loved" is far more in itself than merely an action by God, it is intrinsically incorporated into His very nature and personality itself. Not only does God love but God IS love; He is love personified; it is just that basic!

So as stated previously, that loving is not simply an action, it is the very core of His nature. He "is" love, so He naturally loves so intensely because it is a vital part of His very character. This may sound strange, but actually God has no other choice than to love for that is exactly what He actually is by His very nature.

It was in the eternal Godhead that the very concept of love originated. It certainly was not that we first loved Him, and that He then responded to our love for Him, but instead that He loved us from the start and is now looking for a loving response back from us to His aggressive love for us over the ages. And He has certainly made our responding back to Him for such a love as He has shown to us so very easy for us now to actually do ourselves.

There was no external pressure to force Him to love us. He just loved for He is love. He loved us this very intense way even before creation and then created us to be the actual "target" of that very same love. He loved before Adam's sin and he loved after the rebellion in Eden. He loves today and will love for eternity. That reality is part of His predetermined will, and nothing will ever change that fact in any way whatsoever. We are the central object of that love of His whether we actually want to be so or not.

Satan may have tried to make us unlovable to God, but Satan failed miserably in that endeavor. He really "blew it" badly in that attempt. For instead of causing God to turn away from us because we had there turned away from Him, he actually caused God to come after us aggressively, and in so doing gave us a much greater motivation than ever before for loving Him in return, for we can now see what God's love actually rescued us from, and the extreme to which He went in order to do just that for us.

Satan's worse act of rebellion against God only served to increase our love back to God for His actions, and that latter fact certainly does not make us "unlovable" to God in any way for sure. Instead, it only served to strengthen that two-way love affair from the perspective of our giving of our love back to Him.

He is the sovereign God, and I love the idea that the "Boss" does not need any permission from anyone to do what He wants to do. He just loves, so do not ever try to dispute or deny it. He made the decision, so we accept it and we then take full advantage of that fact for ourselves. The nature of God does not change, and love is what God is by nature, not simply something that He does. It is here to stay, for the eternal God certainly is love beyond any dispute or question whatsoever, and He is certainly "here to stay" Himself.

God knew in advance what that act of loving us would cost Him, yet by a sovereign act of His divine will He determined to love no matter what that cost might be for Him. You see, He felt it was well worth any cost for Him to do so. The treasure was a bride for His Son from "every tribe, nation, tongue and people". And that was certainly well worth any cost or any effort whatsoever on His part to secure for His Son for eternity.

He paid the dowry for a bride for His Son for eternity, with no "separation" or "divorce" possible; for as long as you both shall live, and that is an extended commitment for sure when it relates, as this surely does, to God and us for eternity. There will be no "divorce court" in heaven; the bride and the Groom will be one forever!

The Bible puts it very clearly in a simple, easy to understand illustration. It says in Matthew 13:44 that a man found a treasure hidden in a field, so he sold everything he had to accumulate enough money to be able to buy the whole field in order to get the treasure for himself that was buried there. It is rather a simple story for sure, but nevertheless gives us a beautiful picture of redemption.

There are diamonds in the field so He buys the whole field in order to be able to rightfully have personal ownership of the diamonds for himself that he knows are buried in that field. It is certainly not too difficult to see Calvary's ransom there for sure! He paid for the whole "field" in order for Him to be able to get us for Himself, as we individually respond to His love.

So with God it was a sovereign decision; investing everything in that field in order to be able to get that treasure that He knew was there. He did so because he certainly knew that what was buried there was well worth the cost He had to pay for that whole field in order to get that complete treasure all for Himself. And for that decision of His, and also for the ensuing action that followed that decision He made, we will be eternally thankful.

Does it not make you want to fall before Him with your heart full of thanks for that purchase, and for being willing to personally come up with the entire purchase price Himself? No mortgages on this one; it was paid in full with His own "cash"; the blood of His only Son! Calvary covered the whole cost, so there are certainly no "outstanding balances" still owing here!

He loved us, and yet that love was totally uncaused. If you look up love in a dictionary it will likely say something like this; "The longing, craving, desiring of the heart after something good, desirable or beautiful!" But how about something, wicked, sinful, rebellious or vile?

The dictionary sure does not do justice to that word love when it is God's love to which it refers. For the "good, desirable or beautiful" the dictionary talks about certainly does not describe us before His salvation had wiped us clean in His precious blood, yet we still attracted God's love to us despite that fact.

He loved, yet with nothing desirable within its object or target to attract that love towards it. And that target of His love is unquestionably us. His love for us is so totally uncaused, and yet it still flowing out to us in such abundance. How fortunate we actually are; no need to qualify ourselves for it, and certainly no need to ever question if He loves that vile person we may be standing before at any moment, for there is no need to wonder if anyone qualifies.

None are excluded from His love; it is all inclusive in its total scope. Uncaused; so nobody has to prove themselves worthy of it in any way; even the atheists or the very vilest of sinners are given the same offer and option themselves. One plan and one provision for all, and it is just that simple yet also that all inclusive as well.

As I said earlier, He loves because He loves because He loves. There are absolutely no reasons given us here for that love. It is an uncaused love for certain, but also an uninfluenced one as well. It is not affected by our position in life, or by our social standing. It does not take into account our wealth or lack thereof, and certainly not influenced by political views, economic position or religious affiliation.

It is not affected by any person's beauty or lack thereof; holiness or lack of it; education or wealth or lack of either. It is in no way affected by our race, by the language we speak, by the nationality we consider to be ours, not even by the denominational tag we may wear. There are no barriers and no exceptions. It is a total package for everyone, with nothing extra needing to be added for anyone.

Worship Him or totally reject Him; it will not change that love for us in any way. It is a totally unconditionally, uninfluenced and sovereign love! No wonder we so confidently go to the world with this message of His love for them. Its contents are one hundred percent eternally guaranteed by God Himself and I have a great amount of trust and confidence in any one hundred percent guarantee backed by God! We ourselves may be faithless and unreliable, but not Him. He is always faithful and also totally reliable, and the direction of His love

is totally His own decision, for He alone is totally sovereign

CHAPTER 5

"So Loved" The Spontaneity of His Love

❦

So it should not be any surprise to anyone that we are invited into His actual presence, and certainly so very welcome there as well because of His love. Just imagine a child wondering if it is welcome or even allowed up in mom's arms. Oh, but listen to me wondering child; "Mommy loves you so much! You never need to question whether you are welcome in her arms. If you need her at any time, then just run to her and she will gladly drop whatever she is doing when she sees you coming, just so she can grab you in her arms then hold you tightly."

That is certainly God waiting for us to run to Him as well. Absolutely nothing is of more importance to Him than holding us lovingly in His embrace. Jeremiah 31:3 states; "For I have loved thee with an everlasting love". Run to Him at any time; His arms are always wide open to us. "So thank You, Lord, so very much for holding us so close to Your heart, and never leaving any doubt whatsoever about our being most welcome there at any time."

If you are or ever have been a parent, just think of how you loved (and even still love) that young child, and how thrilled you were to hold the child in your arms. Now multiply that passion a million times over and imagine God's love for us. Yet even then you will not have come close to grasping the full magnitude and scope of that love He has focused upon us.

He so loved us, therefore He could no longer allow Satan to have free access to us, and to continue to allow him to destroy us as Satan was surely already so aggressively doing. Therefore God acted, but certainly radically motivated in that action solely by His love he had for us.

It should not be any surprise that we consequently now serve Him passionately ourselves in return for that love, and that we also now share Him and His love enthusiastically with our world. We surely do have a great story to tell, and tell it out there is something we are certainly going to continue to passionately do for Him.

We have surely found for ourselves the very best there is, and therefore no one should ever be surprised we want to share Him. Why would we ever want to keep the absolute best solely to ourselves? It is not as though there is any limit to the supply of His love that would in any way diminish our personal supply of it by sharing Him with our world. Sharing here is not about "dividing" our limited supply with others. It is instead actually about opening a new limitless supply of His love for all of them personally as well.

God is love and that is one of His very basic characteristics for certain. He is love personified.

His love is the motivation for all of His actions. Nobody has ever run to God for His love, and been refused or even ignored for any reason. So run to Him in confidence with your arms open wide at any time, and there enjoy His wonderful embrace in response, and then listen to Him as He whispers so lovingly to you once again, "I just love you so much and I am so glad to have you again right here with Me!"

No wonder the Father was willing to send His Son, and it is certainly also no wonder that Jesus was so willing to come. No wonder He willingly paid the penalty for every sin we have ever committed, and no wonder He now invites us one and all to take full advantage of that pardon. And it is also no wonder He tells us to share that message of His love with our world, for His passionate love includes them as well in its scope.

It is certainly no wonder as well that He is now very excited, and even so anxious to come back to get us! It is amazing for certain until we begin to understand a little of just how amazing He actually is as such a loving God anyway. Amazing grace; amazing love; amazing pardons; amazing hope and all because He is such an amazing God! To Him be all the glory and all of our praises as well! He certainly is well deserving of it all beyond any doubt.

His love certainly is a very spontaneous love. There is no begging or pleading necessary. Nobody has ever needed to pray, "God, please love me." As stated, there is no asking, begging, pleading or qualifying needed. It is like a child's joy on Christmas morning when they are opening their gifts and they find just the toy they wanted. There is no need to shake the child and say, "You had better be happy with it and love it." The happiness and joy comes spontaneously.

To see that word spontaneous in action just take a glass of water and tip it over, but be sure to do it over a sink because, as you likely already know, there will be no need to shake the glass to get the water to come out. It is going to flow out immediately, naturally, spontaneously with no effort needed to get it to do so. It is just as simple as that to understand God's spontaneous love for us. Just let it flow out to you, and then flow spontaneously over you at all times and in any given situation. But these "glasses" of His love never empty in this case; they just continually keep pouring out to us!

I am getting really serious here now. If you want to understand the word "spontaneous" then you simply take a glass of icy water on a hot, summer day and quickly pour it over your "friend" who is lying there in the sun enjoying its warmth. Then just see how long it takes for them to jump and to say, "BRRRRRRRH!"

I assure you nobody will have to beg or order them to do or say it! What they say and what they then do to you will certainly be very "spontaneous". So sorry, but I just thought that it would be such a "terrific" illustration of the word spontaneous! (PS: Please do not blame me for any adverse consequences to you once you try it!)

You get the point of my lame joke I am sure. But "spontaneous" itself is no "lame joke" when it applies to God's love for us. He loved before we asked for His love, before we knew we needed it, before He even created our original parents and placed them in Eden's beautiful garden, and He still continues to do so even to this very day.

"So Loved" The Spontaneity of His Love

I have often stood at Victoria Falls in Africa on both the Zambian and also the Zimbabwean sides, and in fact I actually lived there on the Zambian side as a missionary for eight months at one time. I have also visited Niagara Falls on both the Canadian and the American sides. They are both amazingly beautiful as the water pours over the lips of these falls, but I am sure I am not surprising anyone by saying this. The water flows over the falls and plunges into the gorges below quite spontaneously. Nobody has to force it to do so; no pumps are required! That is also my word for His love for us; it is spontaneous. It just flows and flows and then flows out some more to us!

Can you not also just imagine God's love flowing out to all of our world in that very same way? So help yourself to all you can use of it in your life and in your family, and then set yourself to sharing it as well with the world! God actually "so loved" it all so very spontaneously.

It is interesting how sometimes we duplicate that little word "so" to radically change its meaning and make it mean something not of any worthwhile significance. We may refer to something as being just "so-so"; somewhat below standard or the expected norm. As you know, it is not a very complimentary compounding of that tiny word "so".

But I am so glad there is only one "so" used here to describe God's love for our world! In fact, maybe it should even have been translated instead here for us as "sooooo loved"! But since there is no adjective in any language capable of fully fathoming and describing God's love, we simply say He "so loved". Even eternity will not see the extent or full dimensions of that word "so" in relationship to

His love. We can just simply continue enjoying His "so" amazing love for ourselves on a daily basis forever.

How is such a love possible? It would be so much easier to understand had it said "so despised" or "so hated" when we consider the rebellion and sin committed against Him by the very object of that love. But He "loved"; now there is something to really "blow your mind". There are no preconditions given here to qualify, such as "if you will do this, then I will love you". It is just a spontaneous love flowing out so very naturally to all of us no matter what our present state of living or even rebellion may be.

I have often prayed for God to save people, heal them or meet many of their needs, but never have I ever prayed for God to love anyone. It flows out naturally and so very spontaneously. No matter whom you stand before, no matter the sin, situation or shame. We can have total confidence in His love as we go to our needy and often very sinful, lost world with its message.

CHAPTER 6

"So Loved"
The Immeasurableness
of His Love

How can we put into words an adequate description of the love of a God of unlimited capacity in any thing He chooses to do? So when He chose to love us, how could such a love possibly be described in words? In fact, John here rightly chooses not to even try to do so, and he simply describes God's motivation as being the fact that He "so" loved, and I fully accept that description of His love for us. We can fill in the blanks for ourselves with any situation or need we face. "So" will cover it all for us no matter what it may be.

This "so" is an extreme even for God. Can you imagine such a reality; an extreme even for God? Stretched to His limit when He has no such limit! It is no wonder we can now feel so safe and so secure in Him. "So" for anyone is an extreme; but a "so" for God; that is an extreme even for the word "extreme" itself! Certainly nothing can compare with that kind of love. Go to the end of your capacity to think "so" and then look even further, because it still stretches ahead of you far beyond the horizons even of your wildest imagination. And that is only the very beginning of His "so loved".

John said "God so LOVED"! What a wonderful word to be taken to such an extreme that it can only be described by using the word "so" to introduce that love to us. Just how much is "SO" anyway? In English it is just a little two-letter word, but when it is placed, as it is in this verse, between God and His love for the world, it becomes in English a tiny two-letter word that is impossible for anyone to measure or even to grasp.

Have you ever seen a mother ask her child, "How much do you really love me"? The child, in response to mom's extremely difficult question, stretches out its tiny arms as far as possible and says, "I love you this much!" The child's tiny arms are stretched out "so" far! In fact they are stretched out as far as the child can possibly reach and likely standing on tiptoe while doing so, with the tiny chest sticking out as far as possible just for a little more emphasis! "That much"! Can you just see the picture?

How much does God love our world? Do you want to stretch out your arms right now as far as you can reach and say, "That much" as well? Wow! How far did you reach? Do you think you stretched them far enough to measure God's "so loved"? I certainly have to admit that I have some serious doubt whether you were able to do so, and do not be in any way offended by my doubting your personal ability on that one. "So loved" is quite a challenge to try to even imagine and certainly quite impossible to measure or demonstrate.

Why does He love us so much? It is certainly a legitimate question here, and I have personally considered that exact same question myself for many years. Yet despite my years of "intense and in depth" thinking on the subject, the very best answer I have been able to come up with to date is to say He loves us because He loves us because He loves us! That is it; nothing we can do to make Him love us any more, and certainly nothing we can do to make Him love us less. He does because He does simply because He does! There is absolutely no further we can take the "why" of His love for us. That is it in total; He does because He does.

It is absolutely futile for us to even try here to grasp the full extent of the why of this love for us. As the old adage goes, "There is no rhyme or reason to it." But when I see Him face to face some day in heaven that question will be at the top of my list, and I will sit with Him for a million years (whatever "years" will mean in heaven) and let Him explain it to me then, and maybe I will then even write another book on it!! And my editor on this one, Cindy McDonald has already agreed to edit it for me, so she is already locked into that deal!!

It is such a wonderful love, so far beyond our imaginations for certain. It will be there, when I see Him face to face that I will then ask God how He could ever have loved me so much. I suspect He will likely just smile at me, and then give me one very big hug! I imagine I will gladly accept that hug as an answer from Him there at that time that will itself explain it all for me forever. After that I will never need to ask Him again, for I will have all the answers that I will ever need to have even for eternity just in that one hug from Him!

The old Sunday school chorus says concerning His love that it is, "Wide, wide as the ocean." As wide as the ocean, and that is beyond doubt certainly wide. I have to admit to that fact for sure. I have flown across the Atlantic, Pacific and Indian Oceans many times over my many years of international travel in world missions, and I can assure you they are each bounded by shores on both sides. They are wide but they certainly have limits to their width despite their size, but His love for our world actually knows no such boundaries. It is unlimited and unbounded.

His love for our world is undeniably unlimited; it knows no limit and it certainly has no "shorelines" either. So this one factor we have to acknowledge, and certainly it is with praise for Him that we do so, is that "so" is "unlimited" when it refers to God's love for us. So we praise Him from hearts filled with genuine love for Him for that wonderful reality of His totally unlimited and unbounded love for us.

Remember as well the chorus about His love for us that says it is; "So high you can't get over it; so low you can't get under it; so wide you can't get around it. Oh wonderful love." None exempted, no matter how wicked or depraved; total universal coverage for all. Worship Him and He will love you. There are certainly no surprises there in that one. But then on the other hand, you may shake your fist in His face and curse His name, and He will also love you. That is "so loved". There are no preset conditions; He just loves us.

In fact, He so loved us so much that He is now so willing to forgive us so many times for so many transgressions because He wants us so much to be with Him for so long; in fact it is for eternity and eternity is certainly so very long for sure! I certainly also do so very much love Him in return, for that very fact that He actually loves me as He does.

An unlimited love! Look up into the heavens some night and have a look at the stars as they glimmer there in the sky, and then remember that many of them are actually bigger than the sun, but because they are so far away from us they are barely visible to us here. Then also remember that the throne room that Jesus left that day to come to a stable in Bethlehem, and then later to a cross in Jerusalem, is well beyond that furthest star, and yet the love that existed there spanned that whole distance to reach out in passion to us.

As you do, try also to imagine the holiness of that home God calls heaven, and then look at the wickedness of our world and imagine the massive gap between these two extremes. Yet His love for this world, and for us as individuals, is unlimited and it easily spans the gap to us on a daily basis as well. I feel it right now even as I sit here and write. It is certainly very warm and comforting; nothing can come close to comparing to it.

That love, originating with God our Creator, is also all inclusive to us today as well. When I was a kid, and that was quite a while ago, we use to sing a chorus in Sunday school that said, "Red and yellow, black and white; they are precious in His sight." (It is probably not even "politically correct" to sing it today.) But it is still true nevertheless. No exceptions; no exemption; none excluded but all are totally included.

We are all in there and God certainly never has seen any difference between us anyway, and for that wonderful fact I am so very thankful. I could not imagine God being affected by any such total nonsense anyway. God did not even make flowers all the same color for sure, and I am actually glad He did not. As they say, "variety is the spice of life!" So there are so exemptions to His love.

Every nation, every race, every color, every language, both male and female, young and old and everyone in between are all included. From the North Pole all the way to the South Pole and back up the other side to the north again. From anywhere eastward or westward whichever way you may choose to go, until you are right back to where you started. There is not one who does not qualify to participate in that love. If you came from the hand of God through our first parents, Adam and Eve, you are in on that love affair and totally included in any offer He has ever made to us based upon that love He has for every one of us.

From Adam to the child being born as you read this page and even after you get into the next chapter, all come into this world fully meeting all the qualifications for being included in that love promise. Christians, Muslims, Buddhists, atheists, idol worshippers or whomever; we can look them all straight in the face and without any hesitation or second guessing whatsoever on our part say confidently to them all, "God loves you!" All are included all the time; none are excluded at any time! Mother Theresa for sure, but also included is the world's worse terrorists as well. The total scope of humanity! It includes all of you for certain and it even also includes me as well.

Go to Niagara Falls with a mug in your hands and fill it with water from the falls. Then look into the mug and ask yourself if you have been "greedy" and as a consequence of your "greed" or your need for water just for yourself, if you have maybe seriously diminished the water supply for Lake Ontario which is just downstream from Niagara or for the St Lawrence River as it flows eastward from that massive lake into the Gulf of St Lawrence and the Atlantic Ocean, just by taking a mug of water from the falls for yourself.

That is God's love. Help yourself to all you need and share it as widely as possible. Nobody will even notice any diminishing of the supply, or have to go without for themselves because of the supply you took for yourself. He just so loves with an unlimited supply available.

CHAPTER 7

"So Loved"
The Passion of His Love

God's love for the world is actually extremely passionate. Of course, as I think about that fact, I am wondering how love could possibly be anything but passionate anyway. It just does not seem logical to imagine a love that is not so. I even love my little dog passionately, and if you do not believe me, then you just try to hurt her while I am around. That is my love for my little dog, but what about God's love for us? Now there is a passionate love for sure.

I hope it is okay if I do use the same word here to try to describe both loves? But our English language, despite its rich vocabulary, still has so very few adjectives that can actually be used here, and even when the most descriptive ones available are used, they fall so far short of painting the actual picture of His love. Maybe that is why John used such a short little word here in this verse between God and His passionate love for the world; "He SO loved", and it is certainly so passionately then expressed that He does love us.

So think passion relating to His love here, and then stretch your imagination to the extreme as far as it will go, and as you do realize that is only "chapter one" of the full story of His love. God certainly does so love us, and he does love us so very passionately.

How passionate would any love have to be to give your son to die for the object of that love? Not only to die, but to be cruelly crucified in shame upon a cross. How about then adding the reality that the object of that love is a sinful, wicked, rebellious world? You give your only Son to die in such agony and shame for such an "unlovable" world. Is "passionate" anything close to being an adequate word to describe such an act?

Do you understand my frustration in trying to describe that simple little two-letter word John used here to try to show us that love? Passionate is all consuming and consequently directs all attentions solely towards the object of that passion. Certainly nothing else at any time ever matters by comparison with the object of that passionate love.

So just how much does God love us? I have to admit that I cannot answer that question! It is beyond understanding, description or even illustration. Even "all of eternity" will not fully reveal or even demonstrate its full extent. And I certainly recognize that the words "all" and "eternity" do not really belong together in any single sentence. His passionate love goes on forever, and then forever again just for emphasis, and that is only the beginning of it.

What is really so fascinating about this passionate love is that it is eternal in both directions; no beginning and no ending! How can our finite minds grasp such a mind boggling concept;

forever in both directions? Yet that is in fact reality in relationship to God's love for us. He always has and certainly always will continue to love us in this very same way. There will be no changes, so have every confidence in it for eternity. It came to us willingly from eternity past before we were even created, and it will continue to be focused upon us for eternity future.

When we think about love it is often self-centred. I love you because I need you and I love what your love does to me, and certainly that is a very real part of it. But then there is a loving where only hatred is returned instead for that love. Now there is quite a different love for sure.

Imagine a parent loving a child who hates them, and gets nothing in return for that love except hurt, embarrassment and heartbreak. That is truly a very passionate love, to love so intently when it actually is only a one-directional love at any time, and so often hatred and rebellion is all that is given back in return to the original lover from that very object of their love.

I am passionately loved by God. I still feel His arms around me today as I write, and I certainly do not expect that wonderful reality to ever change for me. I love being loved by Him for sure, but I also love to be able to love Him in return as well. What a wonderful two-way relationship that makes for both me and also for God Himself, and it is here to stay!

We are definitely "hooked" on such an exciting, eternal love affair as does exist between Himself and us, and I certainly love it beyond description. In fact, what could there ever be about such an amazing love for anyone not to also want to love

Him passionately in return for it? Be loved, then love Him in return, and actually be loved right back by Him so passionately once again!

Can you imagine having to one day face the holy God if He did not love us as we know He actually does? It would be terrifying to say the very least! But now change that picture, and then imagine the day when face to face we meet this passionately loving God for ourselves.

I can just imagine myself also then passionately running to Him with my arms open wide. And as I run to Him, seeing His arms spread out to also welcome me as well as I come to Him. I can hear Him saying to me there with such intense love, "Don't you ever leave my side again! I love you so much I want you to stay close to me forever. Welcome home and you are home to stay!"

This is the love that reached out to me before I was even born. In fact, it actually reached out to me even before creation itself. But it is certainly also the love that reached out to me one Thursday night so many years ago, when as a teenager I fell on my knees before Him at a church altar to give my life to Him forever; from that point onward with no reservations, and also for whatever He willed for me.

It is also the same love that still yearns so passionately even today for the wayward of our world. It reaches out to them in the exact same way as we are presently experiencing His love reaching out also to us personally today.

I feel Him looking me straight in the face even today and saying, "I love you so much". Like a parent looking into the eyes of a child, smiling and saying the exact same words, and then bending over and kissing that child on the cheek. Have you ever personally felt that kiss of love yourself from the Father who so very passionately does love you Himself?

He loves us so much that His attention is focused totally upon us. He created and set up the whole universe to operate "automatically", with total precision within seconds even over many centuries, so that His attention would not need to be taken up with its operations and timing, and consequently He could then concentrate wholly upon us instead. (I had better leave that one alone here before I get into trouble with the astronomers and the theologians.)

That intense love is so comforting, and also such a great source of security for us today. When Satan attacks with his worse assault, we can simply "snuggle" into God's arms and "stick our tongues out at Satan". I admit I have a crazy imagination, but just try it for yourself the next time Satan attacks you. I love sticking my tongue out at him from the safety of God's arms!

God loves us so much that nothing should ever scare or bother us. He loves us so much He will not allow anything that is not totally in line with His will for us to ever touch any of us. I know personally I am part of that world he loves so intensely, and that is certainly the greatest source of comfort and total security that I can even imagine. The confidence of knowing for certain that He loves me that way is surely good enough for me.

While streets of gold, gates of pearl and walls of jasper, surrounding mansions of huge dimensions will be great, His love will be by far the greatest attraction for me for eternity. It is going to be a relationship like we cannot even imagine with the many limitations of this present life, when we can literally feel the warmth of His wonderful embrace for ourselves forever.

Just how all encompassing and how secure is His passionate love for us? Well how much do we need it to be? We can be assured that it is that much for certain, and so very much more than that as well. It is so much that I am confident that when we stand with Him that day, and feel His arms around us, we can be certain that He will have already wiped all our sins from His own memory and also from our memories as well as a result. That is the passionate love He freely offers to us even here in this life at present as well.

"Your love, Lord is a great mystery to me even here and now, but I can only imagine how there must be quite a relationship between us awaiting me at home." And I certainly suspect that is what the whole story of redemption is all about. I enjoy it now for sure, but eternity together in a total relationship of love between us; I can hardly wait for that experience to begin!

I have been loved here for certain in my lifetime, but surely nothing compared to what I expect He has planned for me for eternity. "Lord, I want You to know I will be a willing participant in that future loving relationship. Lord, I will be there at home to meet with You just as soon as my work You have assigned for me to do here is finished and You then call me home."

There will surely be no wanting to wait here for a little while longer on my part before I go to meet Him. That is a fact for sure. I am certainly ready now and also quite eager to meet Him face to face when He is actually ready to take me home with Him.

It is interesting that we usually think of God as One who stands totally self-sufficient; in need of nothing. But I have come to realize that is not the case at all with God. The great God of unlimited creative capability and capacity stands in dire and desperate need of something He could not simply create for Himself, and even today is still unable do so.

That statement may amaze you or even raise a question in your mind, but it is an undeniable fact just the same. You see, He is in great need of our love showered on Him willingly and continuously. That He certainly could not create Himself. For Him to have to force that love from anything or from anyone He created would certainly not be the willing, spontaneous love He so desperately needs from us all today.

He really loves us, and He therefore is also in desperate need for that love to be willingly and abundantly returned to Him by us for eternity, and certainly on a very natural, spontaneous basis for sure. And it is such a great joy for us to be able to do just that for Him on a daily basis.

There certainly is no doubt whatsoever that He surely deserves that love and deep commitment today from every one of us with all the passion we can actually muster in giving it to Him, since He loves us so passionately Himself anyway. If you yourself also want to feel close to God on a daily basis then simply remember this fact, and act daily upon it; God really loves to be loved Himself as well!

If you will say yes to that need, He will "grab" you and wrap His arms around you and hold you to His heart, and will never allow anything or anyone to get close enough to you to ever bring anything into your life without His total permission. Nothing gets pass His arms and close to you, except what He knows will make you stronger, accomplish His divine will for your life, and also in the process make you love Him more than you ever did before. Cherish that fact, and enthusiastically embrace that love for yourself. It is a certain reality and totally yours for the asking at any time.

That love affair He has with us is also so passionate that He can hardly wait to come to get us, and then take us home to Himself forever. We are told that only the Father knows the day of His coming for us, and I can just see Jesus right now "sitting on the edge of His seat" and saying to His Father, "Is it time yet? Can I go get them now? I love them so much I need them here with Me right now!" Or "now now" (manje, manje) as my many African friends like to say for special emphasis. I suspect Jesus is asking the Father right now as well; can I go get them "manje, manje", or if He says it in English then how about "now now"!

We also should be just as excited as He is about our eventually being together forever, and also wondering as well if it is about to happen "now now". But I also fully realize that would be quite a challenge for us to be as excited as He certainly is about our meeting, when He is so much more capable of personally loving us than we are actually capable of loving Him in return at present. But some day! Just wait for God to step up our capacity to love when we see Him that day there

face to face! We will certainly then show God some real love in return for His eternal love to us here.

CHAPTER 8

"So Loved"
The Eternal Aspect
of His Love

Since He is an unchanging, eternal God, He has always loved us, and always with God is certainly a very long time indeed. What you see and experience today is what He always has been, and also will always continue to be. There is "no variableness neither shadow of turning with Him". (James 1:17) He is totally, eternally, one hundred percent consistent. What you see is what you get; now and forever, so rely totally and fearlessly upon this unchanging God, and also upon His unchanging, eternal love; a love that is actually as unchanging and as eternal as God is Himself.

"Loved" is written here in the past tense, but this word "loved", as it here relates to us, is actually eternal; from eternity past, through the present and into eternity future. The Scripture puts it very simply, "I have loved you with an everlasting love". (Jeremiah 31:3) There is certainly no "best before" or "expiry" date on His love! This is absolutely certain for the simple fact that God is eternal and He is also unchanging, so rest assured in His eternal, unchanging love.

God had you and He had me in His omniscient mind from all of eternity already past, and we will stay fixed there for eternity future. Before the first flower bloomed or leaf blew in the breeze; before the first wave rolled upon any shore, and even before the angels began worshipping before His throne, He "so loved" the world. We are safe and oh so secure in that wonderful reality both today and forever!

Our finite, little minds cannot even come close to fathoming "eternal". How can anything be without either beginning or ending? Some day, when we get our new, eternal bodies, our little minds will be greatly expanded in capacity, yet we will likely still be overwhelmed trying to understand His eternal love.

Another amazing reality of God's love for us is the fact that it is an unchanging source of love, and that is such a great source of comfort to us. God is our God on the mountains and He loves us there. We are usually very conscious of His love at these times when things are going well for us in our daily lives.

But He is also our God in the valley and loves us when we are there as well, even when we face trouble, hardships, heartache and many other such negatives. Sometimes there we may even wonder if He actually still does love us as we have to walk through these things, but His love is unchanging no matter what the situation or circumstances may be for us. He is the God of the good times, but He is also the God of the bad times as well, with an unchanging love for us in every situation no matter what we see around us.

Sit in your beautiful church and worship Him and know for certain that He loves you. That is not to difficult to do nor hard to understand. Then go to the other extreme, and this is one which is such a huge reality in many areas of our world today, you may die in your burning church with the doors having been barred from the outside by some religious radicals who have set the church on fire with you helplessly barred inside. Their objective in doing so is simply to destroy you, along with the other members of your church as well who have all assembled there to worship with you, only because you are all followers of Jesus.

Yet God's love is still one hundred percent for you even in that situation as well, but it is not only for you and His other followers who came to worship Him in that church with you, and are now instead dying extremely painful deaths because of being there, but and this is quite a mind boggling reality, His love is also still one hundred percent for the ones who lit the fires and are yelling insults at Jesus and His dying followers from the outside as well.

So we love our enemies and pray for those who persecute Christians because God also loves them as much as he loves us, no matter what they may do to His followers. These terrible acts they are committing, actually on their own, change absolutely nothing in relationship to God still loving them. There is nothing any radical or terrorist can do to diminish God's love for them in any way. It is "locked" on them no matter what they may do!

God loves me here in my safe office as I write, but He equally loves my brothers or sisters in prisons in many countries; imprisoned there simply because they are serving Him and certainly for no other reason. But again He also loves the guy who turned the key on their cell door to lock them inside, and even the ones who sent them there because of their religious hatred of Christians as well.

Perhaps we all need to sit in a prison cell for a few years in solitude with no trial, guilty of only one "crime", and that crime being the fact we have chosen to be a follower of Jesus, to get to really know a little more of His love; "unchanging" no matter what the circumstances! I am sure the early church, and especially the disciples who all died violent deaths, except John who was instead exiled to the tiny island of Patmos, recognized His unchanging love for them even as they were being stoned, beheaded or themselves crucified for serving that very One that they knew loved them.

Tradition says that Peter was likely crucified head down because he did not feel worthy to die in the same way the Savior who loved him so much had Himself died for him, and whom Peter also so passionately loved as he hung there dying himself years later.

The old hymn states so forcefully that "His love hath no limit, His grace hath no measure, His power no boundaries known unto man. But out of His infinite riches in Jesus He giveth and giveth and giveth again" Yet His giving of His love to any or all of us does not in way diminish that unlimited supply of love for the world. He loved when there were only two; Adam and Eve, and He still loves today with billions of people with still no sign of any limit whatsoever to His love supply in sight as yet!

We are so conscious of His love as we enjoy our lives in serving Him in good health, but we may be suffering terrible pain and dying from some incurable disease as well, and still know His love for us has not changed in any way.

As mentioned earlier we try to illustrate this fact to kids when we teach them to sing that it is as wide as the ocean and also as deep as the sea. It may be the best illustration we can come up with for them, but it certainly does not come close to doing His love justice.

So drink deeply from that unlimited supply of the fountain of His love, and then tilt your head back, open your eyes as wide as possible and look out upon the entire world, and then realize that the unlimited supply of love that you are "drinking" from for yourself is also equally available to the whole world without in any way diminishing what is available to you.

CHAPTER 9

"The World" The Total Range of His Love

He so loved "the world", but as previously stated, the immensity of that object of His love does not in any way minimize my share of that love He has personally for me. His love for me, while it is so great, is simply a spoonful of water dipped from the ocean compared to the total supply available for the world.

God wrapped His arms around the whole world and said "I love you", and now He also wraps them around each of us individually and says it again. So the "so loved the world" is both collective as well as individual; it includes everybody but also certainly includes anybody in its scope as well. We are therefore included in His love whether we even want to be there or not. There is no escape route from it for anyone.

I have often been amazed by the fact that "so loved" did not also include the fallen angels as well. Amazingly, it only included our race from Eden's origin in its scope. Despite the fact that the fallen angels were originally with God in heaven when they rebelled, and were consequently expelled, we are told nothing of His still loving them, and doing anything to try to bring them back to Himself. His love was instead focused totally upon us, and has remained exclusively there to this very day.

It is certainly a fact that this love affair only applies to us as His created beings from Eden. It was this very creation of God that Satan led into an open rebellion against our Maker there that day, and it surely does now include all of us that fit that description.

Yet with us it was so very different, and I am thrilled by that fact. He became the "aggressor" and went after us as His "lost sheep" on the dangerous mountains, and I am now so very thankful that He actually did just that for us. It is so great to now be a "found sheep" instead of still being one of the lost ones.

He did find His lost sheep because He so aggressively went after them despite the "life-threatening" hazards He had to face in order to successfully accomplish this feat. These dangers did not matter in any way to the Shepherd, for His sheep desperately needed Him there to help them! The dangers and the hazards of the mountains mean very little to the shepherd when his sheep are lost in them, and consequently in serious personal danger themselves.

I am so glad He actually made an exception for us, and that He did not treat us as He did these fallen angels, whom He left to simply perish. Consequently He actually did set up a "second chance" option for all of us instead. As a result of that divine exception He made for us, things are now so very different for "the world", His Eden creation, than what they are for the fallen angels from heaven.

I am sure He also loved the trees, the flowers and the lakes, rivers and mountains He had created as well, but the concentration of His passionate love was totally upon us, collectively referred to here as "the world", and I am so happy to personally also be included in that wonderful, all inclusive word for certain.

"The world" is certainly such an all inclusive expression. I have sometimes even wanted to ask God if He loves everyone the way He loves me, especially when I see the wickedness around me, but then I am brought back once again to this little expression, and I hear Him say to me anew; "Remember I love the whole world and absolutely nobody is excluded". This is certainly a one hundred percent all inclusive deal to us from God Himself, and you are just not anywhere going to get any better deal than that.

We all know how it feels to love someone who also loves us right back in the same way, but have you ever passionately loved someone who hated you? The child says, "I hate both of you!" But you still continue to love that child. There is a difficult love for sure, but that is God's love for so much of our world; one-sided, scorned, denied, rejected or totally ignored and unwanted, yet still so very real.

Such continued rejection must really break His heart even today. The most rebellious part of His whole creation on this earth is the one part of that creation He surely loves the most, and that number one object of His passionate love is certainly us for sure. That fact is really totally beyond dispute.

Of course, it was for that very reason that Satan turned his full, vicious attention upon us. He wanted to cause God the most hurt and anxiety he could possibly bring to the God, who had expelled him and his fallen angels out of heaven. He therefore went after the primary target of God's love, and Satan had no doubt whatsoever that surely it was us.

As a result, Satan made us the priority target of his efforts to continue and even expand that rebellion he had led against God in heaven itself. So God was actually Satan's primary target when he went after Adam and Eve in Eden. He just wanted to try to get even with God by destroying our side of this relationship of love with God.

That is why I love to shake my fist in Satan's face and say, "You lost it with me!" And I certainly do not need to explain the "it" to Satan for sure. He knows exactly what I am referring to, for he surely will never forget his personal rebellion against God, and what it actually did to him and to his evil followers for time and for eternity.

His very worse act of rebellion and treason against God, and then later towards us, only served to show us God's love for us more clearly than ever we could otherwise have known it. Satan certainly "shot himself in the foot" as the old saying goes, because his very worse act of treason against God instead served to show us the very best act of God's love for us.

I guess there is no need to even say this here, but I will add it anyway. "No matter who you are, where you live, how holy or how sinful you may have been or even presently are, no matter what nationality you call yourself or what language you speak, God loves you." A pretty simple fact for anyone to grasp for certain, but also an exciting reality for the whole world to revel in as well!

"God so loved the world." But have you heard any of the world's many stories in their response to that love? Actually there are countless thousands of them, but here are just a few of them that come to mind as I write.

There once was a man named Saul, which is of course a very common name, so that is not much of a clue for you as to whom I am referring. But this one Saul had set as his priority in life the task to try to destroy as much of the church of his day as possible. I suspect you may now have heard of this particular Saul to whom I am referring. If not, then you can read about him in Acts 8:3 and also 9:1-6.

Yet God loved him despite his ungodly objective, and actually took the time to stop him "in his tracks" one day on a road leading to a town called Damascus to have a private "chat" with him right there on the roadside where he had fallen to the ground. In fact, it was actually God who knocked him to the ground to keep him there while He talked with Saul.

You very likely now know the story of what then happened to Saul as God's love reached out to him and then moved totally into his life. Actually Saul never "recovered" from that encounter with God that day. It changed his life so very radically, and it even changed his name from Saul to Paul, although that last change does not happen to everyone! It was, in that case, certainly an exception to the norm to get a name change from a personal, life-changing encounter with God. But the transformation was nevertheless quite radical for him for certain.

In fact, he later even became an apostle and also wrote more of the New Testament than any other writer. That is just one story among so many of God's reaching out in love to the world He so loved, and in that action bringing about an amazing transformation in the process.

I do not have the space to tell this story in any detail of a young street gang dope dealer name Nicky Cruz who was one of the first converts of David Wilkerson's then newly organized ministry called Teen Challenge. Nicky Cruz met Jesus one day and fell totally for the love Jesus then offered to him. It changed his life to the point where he became one of the biggest promoters of God's love for the street gangs and dope addicts in New York City, and then later throughout the whole continent.

His story later became quite familiar to millions as he was the central person whose story was featured in David Wilkerson's best selling book, "The Cross and the Switchblade". God's love, once accepted and applied to an individual life, still continues to work such miracles of transformation in lives around our world even to this day.

These kinds of stories have been repeated millions of times over because of God so loving the world that they could not resist His love for them individually. It changed their lives once they personally accepted that love, and then sent them into the world with that same life-transforming message for others as well. Such stories continue even today on a daily basis.

There is certainly no account anywhere on record of anyone ever, at the end of their life, expressing regret that they accepted that love God offered to them, and their reaching out to have it for themselves. But there sure are millions of positive ones being repeated out there!

Sometimes we easily stand in awe of that love for the world as it is demonstrated, but there are other times when it takes a great deal of contemplating on our part to be awed by it in some other specific situations. In fact, we may actually have some serious questions about that love instead, until we actually know the whole story. I want to take a few minutes here to also talk a little about God's world love affair from that often confusing perspective as well.

In the mid 1950's five young men got the attention of this continent, and they also got my attention a few years later as well when their story was written. They were five American missionaries in Ecuador, South America. Their names were Jim Elliot, Nate Saint, Pete Fleming, Ed McCully and Roger Youderian.

These five guys had set as their mission goal the task to reach a tribe of Indians in Ecuador who had never been touched by the Gospel previously. The tribe was called the Aucas. They were violent and very unapproachable by anyone from outside the tribe at that time, but these guys recognized they were certainly part of God's worldwide love affair, and as such they determined to reach them with that love.

To do so the five of them decided to become a team, and together then to go into the deep jungles where the tribe lived hidden from any outside contact, with their objective obviously being to try to reach the tribe with the message of God's love.

Their story was later told in Elizabeth Elliot's well known book "Through Gates of Splendor" which many thousands have certainly read over the years since she first wrote it, and it actually became an almost immediate bestseller in the field of Christian books.

One of these five guys was Nate Saint. Nate flew a small pontoon plane in his ministry in Ecuador's jungles. So for months these five guys flew over that tribe, and the area of that jungle where they lived, hidden from any outside contact. As these missionaries did so, they dropped gifts and also tracts to these Aucas. They even dropped pictures of themselves with the little plane, hoping it would help to have them recognized by the Aucas when a face to face meeting would eventually take place.

After some time doing so, they felt it was then time for that meeting, so they flew in, landed the little plane on a river, brought it ashore and waited. Their wives waited nervously at home; and the women waited, and waited! But the five wives heard nothing from their husbands for several days.

A number of days later a search plane was sent into the jungle to look for them, and they finally found all five of these guys dead on the river bank near their plane. Nate Saint, the pilot, had a spear through his body with a gospel tract he had dropped from his plane to the Aucas wrapped around that spear shaft. They had wrapped his Gospel message he had dropped to them around the very weapon they used to kill him.

Five young missionaries dead there that day without having won a single convert in the tribe they had set about to reach with this message of God's love for them. Murdered by the very people they had gone lovingly themselves to try to share God's love with and hoping to win.

Does such a seeming tragic event make you wonder about this love affair, and question why God did not intervene there in some way so these missionaries could somehow have reached them? If that question is there in your thinking in any way, then just wait for the remainder of the story before you draw any conclusions on the chain of events, and God's love for the world shown even here for this tribe and also for the world in the process.

The news media immediately picked up the story and as a result the Auca tribe became the prayer focus of thousands of Christians. The Holy Spirit then began to mysteriously work among the Aucas, and soon a friendly contact was made with that same tribe, and eventually Nate Saint's sister, Rachael, and also Elizabeth Elliot, the wife of another of the five, Jim Elliot, themselves went back into that tribal area to minister to the Aucas.

A number of years later these two women walked unto the platform of a Billy Graham crusade in West Berlin accompanied by two of the warriors who had actually killed these missionaries, to report that practically the whole tribe had become Christians by that time. Five missionary lives that eventually saw almost a whole tribe come to Jesus!

So I ask the simple question here; does God know what He is doing? I strongly suspect that He actually does know for sure! In fact, God took Satan's worse and used it to attract so much of the prayer attention of the church towards that tribe, that His will was certainly eventually accomplished for the tribe, and likely far beyond what any of the original five missionaries could have even dreamed.

I can just imagine the "hugging" in heaven when these converted warriors eventually met these five missionaries there face to face!

Later Elizabeth Elliot wrote two books on these missionaries. One called "Shadow of the Almighty", and the other as already mentioned called "Through Gates of Splendor", and Rachael Saint also wrote one on her brother, Nate, called "Jungle Pilot" I have had all three of these great biographies in my personal library for about fifty years.

Reading these books was really my first serious and by far my greatest direct confrontation with a call to missions in my own life as a young Christian at that time, and I never got away from that calling. I responded to the challenge and went to Africa as a missionary a number of years later, but so also did many hundreds of other young people as well for about a whole generation. Hundreds of them personally heard God's calling to them to some distant mission field as a result of hearing and then later reading the story of these Gospel martyrs, and as a result became missionaries themselves to nations all over the world!

So dare I to ask the same question a second time here? Does God actually know what He is doing? What do you think? Did God "slip up" with these five guys and let Satan destroy their ministry? I seriously think not! Actually it makes me want to laugh in Satan's face again! What God was actually doing in these five lives that He allowed to be killed on the distant river bank that day was sharing His love "for" the world "with" the world through increasing His outreach force by thousands around the world. You lost another one for certain, Satan and a big laugh at you again!

That is the "big picture" as God sees it. He is in love with the whole world, and certainly He has great plans to let that fact be known out there, and when we personally make ourselves available to Him to help Him accomplish that reality, He then takes our commitment to Him and also to the world He loves so very seriously indeed.

Later I heard Elizabeth Elliot speaking in person at Wheaton College in the USA at a world missions gathering I was attending there in the late 1980's. This statement of hers that she made there has stayed with me since that day. She stated, "Jim Elliot did not die in Ecuador. That is actually only where they later found his body! Instead Jim died one night at an altar while still a student at Wheaton College, when he bowed before God that night and said, Lord, my life no longer belongs to Jim Elliot. From here onward my life belongs totally to Jesus Christ!" She continued by then adding, "That is where Jim really died. The jungles of Ecuador are only where they later actually found his body!"

He so loved the world, that He continually works His plan to bring as many as possible into His arms. Sometimes we do struggle to understand the mysteries of His amazing ways of working. But someday we will see it all even as He now sees it so clearly Himself already. So let it be; no more questions here from us. "God we know that You love the world, so we are ready to say amen to any decision You now make to ensure the world hears of Your great love for them."

"God so loved the world!" It is imperative we keep this reality central in our thinking and living at all times. Otherwise we may sometimes question

God's often mysterious ways of working with that love affair He has both for and also with the world.

As I sit here and write tonight there is a calendar hanging right beside me. I see on it that tomorrow is actually October 5th and you may say, "So what". Well here is the "so what". It was October 5th in 1988 that our son, Darryn, died instantly of a massive heart attack going in through the church door at our home church at that time in Grand Falls, Newfoundland, Canada.

We had returned to Canada from Africa a year earlier, and it was only after we returned and went for standard medical tests, as is common after an extended period of time overseas, that his problem was discovered. We had consequently known for about a year after coming home from Zambia that he had this very serious heart problem, and as a result he had been grounded; no running, swimming or playing games.

His classmates at school privately, with the teacher's permission, set up a schedule among themselves to play chess with him during gym classes because he was not allowed to do any exercises whatsoever, and they did not want him to be left alone during these gym classes. It was only after his death that we actually found out what the students were doing for him.

We were living at that time just two houses from the church we attended, so on that Wednesday night he left to walk over to the church to help his youth group prepare to host a youth convention that coming weekend which was Canadian Thanksgiving. Going in through the church door he collapsed before he was even fully inside with his feet were still outside, and it was there that he died instantly of a heart rupture. He had turned fifteen just ten days earlier.

The Saturday afternoon service at that youth convention that weekend was his funeral service. He had been born in Zambia during our first term there and lived there for a number of years. Just prior to coming home from Zambia that last term before he died, I had arranged, as our mission's field director for Zambia, the purchase of a one hundred and seventy-six acre property near Kitwe with about ten buildings on it, on which the Trans Africa Theological College currently operates as well as the location for the present Kitwe Village of Hope children's homes. Darryn had lived in that same city of Kitwe for about the first two years of his life and on our second term to Zambia he had lived in Lusaka.

The college there on that site had no chapel at the time of Darryn's death so we made the decision to make that the project at his funeral service, and they set up donation tables there at the church for us for his funeral. As a result, the youth who were attending that convention, as well as our own family and friends donated enough money to build a chapel at that college for the ministry students there to be able to use.

Over the last 25 years as I now write this, hundreds of Zambians, in training for ministry to Zambia and to the other nations of Africa have worshipped, prayed, sought God's will and made life commitments to minister His love to their world right there in that memorial chapel, and have then gone out of that college to take their nations for God, getting close to 2,000 churches in the national church we worked with, just in that one nation

"The World" The Total Range of His Love

of Zambia at the time of my writing this account, and it is just beginning to really explode in growth nationwide. An interesting factor for me and my family is that the vast majority of these pastors have been actually trained at that college and while there worshipped and prayed in that very chapel.

So, simply stated, if that is what God wanted from Darryn and our family (and I am sure it is) then there has never been any "why God" from us on the whole matter. It is totally in His reliable hands at all times! He loves "the world' and when we make ourselves available to his plan to share that love, He takes that commitment very seriously, but we can be very assured He also keeps great records for us for eternity as well,

For God so loved the whole world, but that all-inclusive fact does not make me "jealous" in any way. In fact, I am delighted that the word loved is actually shared with the world, and I am sure it is because of that very reason that God has impressed the world so heavily upon my own heart through most of my life. It is because He also wants me to simply be a channel for that love to flow out to the world, and I have gladly accepted that challenge myself over the years, and it has been such a privilege to do so.

"The world" I look at my neighbors across the street, and I look at my friends around the world. I look at the nations from Afghanistan and Albania to Zimbabwe and Zambia, and every other nation between from A to Z and I know they are all the targets of His love. The world He so loved is every nation, over every generation. So the challenge continues for us even today.

North America and Europe are usually placed at the top of world maps, but that is not the way God sees the world, and I am quite certain you realize that fact. We at the "top of the map" are not His exclusive priority for sure. We are simply part of His total priority, and I bless Him for that wonderful reality. In fact, I have heard it said that the most important people in the whole world to God could very well be those who have never yet heard of His love for them. They are certainly the priority of His outreach love today, and they surely need to be at the very top of our priority list as well.

"So loved the world!" so what do I do about that amazing fact? Well, what did God Himself do about that love? As we have a detailed look at His actions in relationship to that fact, then maybe we need to react to that joyous reality of His love for the world in the same way as He did. We will now have a serious look in the next chapter at just what He actually did do for us as a result of that love for the world. God responding to us in total love can certainly be an extremely exciting reality.

CHAPTER 10

"THAT HE GAVE" THE AMAZING ACTION OF HIS LOVE

"That He gave". Now there is a Giver with some giving potential for sure! The Creator, who in a mere six days spoke the entire universe into existence, gave a gift to the world to precisely express His passionate love for us. Yet even the whole of creation is never once referred to by God as a gift to us because of His love for us. So it was a gift that even eclipsed creation, as wonderful as that was in the beginning. Yet this one act of giving outshone all others, for this act of giving was intended to show us clearly His intense love for us.

Here was quite a challenge even for God. Whatever could it possibly be that He gave as a result of that love He most certainly had for us, that would be capable of showing that love to us? Could God have simply created another world, or even another universe as a gift?

Yet if He had done so that would only have taken a few words for Him to speak into existence, and a mere moment of His time to make it happen, and such a gift would have been there instantly for us. It would have taken very little effort and absolutely no cost to Him to make it happen. Certainly if he had done so, it would have been considered a cheap gift, since it was coming from the One with such creative capacity, and actually costing Him absolutely nothing in the process to make it available to us.

A giving God should certainly not be any surprise to anyone who recognizes His love. After all, everything we see and have around us is a gift from God. The air we breathe, the planet we live on, the sun that warms us, the food we eat and the water we drink, combined with a million other things are all gifts to us from God. But it is only when we see this specific Gift which He here gave, and then realize its actual cost to God, that we stand so amazed by this one outstanding and amazing act of His giving in love for us.

For this one act of His giving on this very specific occasion had to be different, because the giving of this Gift was prompted, and also motivated totally, by the Givers love for us. So quite naturally our expectations relating to this act of His giving have been raised considerably by that very fact. It will be an exceptional gift for certain, and that expectation is certainly not merely an exaggerated one on our part. Who could ever "exaggerate" their thinking to that extent anyway, unless it was based on such very strong evidence that He actually did love us just that radically anyway.

The Gift was far more than anyone could ever have hoped for or expected when our open rebellion against God is considered in the equation, but we have been told here that the Gift was given to us because He loved us so much, and consequently He had to help us. That wonderful fact should certainly serve to raise our expectations rather high relating to His Gift!

Don't blame your child for getting excited about your gift to him for his birthday, if you are telling the child how much you love him there as you are giving him the gift. It is your expression of your love for the child that is actually to "blame" for the increased expectation and excitement about the gift that is about to be opened! And so it is with us here in this verse. So you can simply "blame" God for our excitement over His Gift to us, since He is the One who started it all and told us that he loved us.

So John tells us that God "so loved" us, and then begins immediately to talk about that Lover giving a Gift to the object of that very love. No wonder our expectations have been soaring here at the very thought of His actual giving of that Gift to us.

So we are told here "that He gave". Note it does not say that He asked us to give, or to do any kind of penance, or any other such thing to earn His forgiveness and pardon. Instead He made the move Himself to become the Giver both to us, and also for us! That is one reality that makes His love for us so believable. He did not simply tell us He loved us. As the old saying goes, "talk is cheap", but there was certainly nothing cheap about this talk, for God acted fully upon what He was actually saying to us.

He gave enough to fully back His talk beyond any doubt from us whatsoever. He acted upon it, and thereby demonstrated it for us by this actual act of His giving. He is a "giving" God as opposed to a "demanding" God, and what an amazingly generous, giving God we actually do serve. It was the ultimate Gift coming from the ultimate Giver!

Looking around me at what He has already given to us in creation, I become very excited when God begins to zero in on just one Gift that is designed to fully demonstrate beyond anything else He ever gave the extent of His love for us. Mom gives her child a cookie now and then but she also would likely give one to his friend who is with him as well, and maybe even a bite for the dog as well. As tasty as the cookie may be, it does not show the extent of mom's love for her child for sure.

But on Christmas morning the gift is not merely a cookie. It is a brand new, ten speed bike because she loves him so much. That is the difference between the gift of creation and the Gift John, in the Scripture we are here referring to, is about to open for us from God.

Actually I can hardly wait for "Christmas morning" to come so I can open that Gift and then see what it actually was that God gave me because He really loved me so much! That is what giving is meant to do for sure. So get all excited, for He is giving us a Gift that certainly has been remembered above all other gifts over the many centuries since He did so.

He saw our desperate situation and gave to rescue us when we could do absolutely nothing to help ourselves, and His giving of that Gift has made an eternal difference for countless millions around our world today, and also many millions more down through the ages as well, and it will continue to make a dramatic difference for us for eternity.

The Biblical story of the prodigal son returning home to his father clearly shows us that his father must have really loved him despite the son's wayward actions, because he obviously was constantly looking down that dusty road for his son to return. It says in Luke 15:20 "But when he was yet a great way off, his father saw him and had compassion, and ran, and fell on his neck and kissed him." He had been watching that road every day since his son left home, and this is just what he was waiting to someday see.

I can just imagine that father standing on the front steps every day looking down the long, lonely road, just watching for his son to hopefully return. And then he finally saw him one day while the son was still a long way down that road leading towards home, so quite naturally he ran excitedly to him. It was all forgiveness from the father towards his wayward son from that point onward. His father never once called him a "prodigal". It is certainly wonderful to have such a loving Father who so willingly forgives beyond anything we can even ask or expect from Him.

The prodigal son talked to his father about becoming one of his "hired servants", but the father was in no way interested in any such employment arrangement. Instead the father gave him a ring, a clean robe and a welcome-home party and then enthusiastically introduced him to the party guests who had assembled as, "my son who was lost but is now found".

So reaching inside Himself, God found a Gift that would completely express His feelings for us, His lost sons and daughters, and He then willingly gave it to us. What a Gift it must have been that He actually had to reach inside Himself to get it, and since that act of giving nobody has ever been able to honestly question the love that prompted such a costly Gift.

We surely serve a giving God! This Gift certainly was not any "Boxing Day sale" item to get rid of surplus supplies. This was a "full price purchase" by God, with no half price sales slip attached to it for certain. This Gift surely did cost God "everything" to give, because it was so very costly indeed for Him to provide the Gift for us anyway! In fact, God could "afford" no greater Gift than the one that He gave.

How does a God who only has to speak anything he wishes or wants into existence, and it is right there, give anything to prove His love that is actually worthy of its source, when that Source is the Creator Himself? Practically any gift He could give would be similar to a millionaire tossing a coin to a hungry child who is begging on the street as he walks by! The coin he simply tosses to the street sure does not cost him anything to give it to that child. It was certainly not much of a "gift"! In fact, it would more likely be simply a reflex action, or worse still, given as an insult in a "now get out of my way, kid" kind of gesture!

However, when God gave us His Gift there certainly was no such attitude involved. The attitude behind His Gift was far closer to a "come here to Me, and let Me hold you" one instead!

This act of giving, and the actual Gift itself, was so amazing and so spectacular, it was and has continued to still be, the main topic of constant conversations around the whole world for the last two thousand years. God found a Gift that has totally amazed the world since it was given so long ago, and has left us with "our mouths wide open" in awe since that Gift was put on view for the world to see! So it surely must have been quite a gift, considering the source and the message it was meant to convey so clearly to us, who are the actual fortunate recipients of that wonderful Gift from Him!

Love is naturally both about "giving" as well as being about "receiving". Love "demands" giving from its source towards its object, yet it is certainly not a forced giving in any way. The "demands" of love refers instead to a pressure inside the giver himself, and the giver's love demands it be given to the object in its focus. It just cannot continue to exist in the source itself without doing just that towards the actual target of that love, whether it is then actually received or even rejected by that target.

The "demands of loving" are actually much more like magnets than being legal demands. The "demands" are simply impossible for the giver to resist. Nobody orders or commands the metal to move to the magnet; it is naturally drawn to it by its very presence and attracting power. So are also the "demands" of loving; not orders but attractions! It is a natural out flowing that is almost impossible to restrain or resist, and certainly who would ever want to resist its attracting capacity anyway? To be loved is wonderful, and I actually love to be so loved myself!

Yet it certainly was not a reluctant giving on God's part for sure. It was instead a giving done in total joy and delight, despite the high cost and the terrible pain it must have cost Him to do so. On that basis God was indeed "forced" to give, simply because His love was so great for the object of that Gift. The magnet just could not be resisted! So He did what He had to do; He gave! He simply had no other choice other than to do just that for us.

"Thank you, God, for such a love that You did actually have to give!" Where would we ever be today if it were not for Your passionate love for us that prompted that giving? We are all so very glad that You did give, and we daily marvel at the effectiveness of that giving of that Gift in our lives even two thousand years later. That was quite a Gift You gave to us, God! We will continue to thank You for that Gift through eternity, and even then will still feel we owe you many more thanks for it!"

"I love you", the Creator said as He gave the Gift, and He still continues to say it today to the whole world. "You are the very passion of My heart; it throbs only for a close relationship with you! Nothing I have ever created comes close to being the object of My love the way you do, so that is why I am giving you the greatest gift that I could ever personally give; the very best that heaven, with all its resources, has to offer to you: the best I can ever afford! Even though it is costing me everything, I am still going to give you this Gift because you also mean everything to Me as well, so what else can I possibly do?"

Don't you just love an Almighty God that actually thinks and also acts that way toward us!

"That He gave" a Gift that cost Him everything, despite the unlimited resources at the disposal of the Creator. The God who owns everything gave "everything" as a Gift to us when He reached inside Himself and gave us that Gift as an expression of His love for us. It really boggles the mind for sure, and I love that very fact that it actually does so. No wonder the hymn writer many years ago wrote, "I stand amazed in the presence of Jesus the Nazarene, and wonder how He could love me; a sinner condemned, unclean."

A Gift that cost the Creator of everything absolutely everything to give is actually quite a Gift indeed! You see God is not caught in a love affair that he is now sorry He ever got involved in anyway, as so many people find themselves seriously involved in around us today. Love can actually bring so much pleasure, fulfillment and happiness as it blooms, and is mutually enjoyed and shared in both directions. That fact I do not need to take the time to explain here for certain.

Unfortunately, and our society knows this reality far too well today, for love does not always remain two-directional. When it ceases to be so, it is then that the pleasure, fulfillment and happiness just mentioned above actually become hurt, confusion and grief instead. One, or usually both of the original "lovers" then wish they had never even originally met and fallen in love, and consequently made such commitments to each other that were certainly originally intended to last a lifetime.

God knew from the very beginning the future results of that Eden love affair, and He also knew in advance the total cost that it would be to Him to love us in that way. He knew as well the Gift He would have to give because of that love, and even the extent to which He would have to give that costly Gift in order for it to restore the broken love relationship between His creation and Himself. Yet His foreknowledge of these events and costs involved did not deter Him in any way whatsoever. He still created, He still loved and He also paid the total price to redeem us anyway!

His first move was to give that Gift to a virgin in Bethlehem to raise in poverty, and then later to exile to a foreign land for a period of time as Herod sought to destroy the One he felt could possibly one day become a threat to his own wicked regime. (Matthew 2:13) So He became a refugee in Egypt from the very beginning of His short earthly life among us. Therefore this amazing act of giving began for God as He initiated the process of expressing His love for us, and then reclaiming us for Himself by restoring that once broken relationship.

But the giving of the Gift went much further even than that, and He knew in advance before He started the process, just how far that giving of that Gift would actually have to go to accomplish its original intent for total restoration.. For Calvary was certainly not a surprise to God! It was instead the original intent, and also the extent of the giving of the Gift of His Son anyway. His Gift was the true Gift that just keeps on giving!

So what is the world worth to God? We need only to have a look at the Gift Itself to see the answer to that question, and yet it is still far beyond our capacity to understand the cost to a loving Father of the giving of that wonderful Gift! The closer we look, and the deeper we dig into the actual process of the giving, the less we understand of its total magnitude and scope. He certainly was a Gift worthy of its source even when that source was God Himself! That is quite a challenge for anyone to ever try to grasp or understand.

He loved intensely, so as a result of that love, He was compelled to give radically. For how can real love look upon any genuine, serious need in its object, and then having the capacity to meet that need, whatever the cost may be, walk away without doing anything whatsoever about that need?

I have a picture saved on my computer that won the Pulitzer Prize for photography some years ago. The picture was taken in 1994 by Kevin Carter, a professional photographer working in the Sudan in northeast Africa during one of its worse famines and civil wars.

The picture is of a little boy, probably about four years old, but his desperate physical condition makes it difficult to judge his actual age. The child is on the ground, too weak to stand or even to crawl. He is nothing except skin stretched over a tiny bony skeleton. This was a very common site there at that time, and still is today in fact, but what also captured the world's attention in that photo was a large vulture standing patiently in the background, just a very short distance from the starving child, waiting for the little one to die so it could eat what was left of the child; actually mostly just skin and bones.

There was a UN feeding station only a couple kilometers away, but it was obvious the child would be a meal for the vulture before he would ever get to the feeding station on his own to eat for himself. So the picture was taken and received a great deal of attention in the western world. So why then have I inserted this story here at this time?

Well here is the real tragedy. The photographer and his team took the picture and published it, but when he was later asked how he had helped the child, he had to admit he had done absolutely nothing; he had simply walked away to look for other pictures, and left the child there on the ground soon to die and then become a meal for a hungry vulture.

He was so criticized for this lack of action on his part, that within three months after taking that picture the photographer himself committed suicide because of severe personal depression; he just could not take the criticism and personal guilt of his lack of action any longer, so he ended his own life.

I am sure you understand fully when I say that I am so glad God did not simply look at us for a "few minutes" in our own desperate need and then simply "walk away"! Certainly the picture John shows us here goes so much further than that. He really did get personally involved in our needs, and then set about to do His utmost to help us with them.

But before we get too personally critical of the apathy of that photographer mentioned here, we need to evaluate our own reactions in many ways as well. Firstly, these kinds of needs are still out there even if we are not standing directly in front of them, so how do we ourselves react to that fact? Do we get directly involved ourselves in dealing with these tragedies from the bountiful supply of our own resources which God has given to us, or do we also just walk away and do nothing?

Secondly there is the greater need that far exceeds this first one stated here; that is the need to get involved in sharing the story of God's world love affair that is so desperately needed out there in our world today. Are we walking away there as well? If so, how do we then differ from that photographer if we are also walking away from the need? God certainly differs Himself a great deal, and has proven it, but how about us? Are we also ignoring instead of going to the need to help?

What an example for us also today in responding to a needy world! If we love Him, then we cannot help but also love the object of His love as well. Then, if we also do love that same object that His love is focused upon, we will also give in many ways so that the world will surely hear of His love. As we do so, our world will then be given the opportunity to respond themselves to that love, and also for them to then love Him in return for His great love shown to them. It will produce positive results in both directions; they will be saved and also God will be loved even more than before.

Reaching inside Himself He gave everything because of that love. Personally I want to get as close as possible to that same commitment to the world, and just give and give and give to reach it with the message of His love.

Certainly the most fulfilling gift we can give back to God, and also to the world for that very same purpose, is to give ourselves; totally, and for whatever He chooses to use that personal gift of ourselves to accomplish for Himself and for His cause. He surely needs the world back in His arms and our giving is certainly designed and intended to accomplish that very purpose.

"God gave", and certainly this very action is something to be thankful for and appreciate! The transgressor is given a gift in love from the One the transgression was against, and that fact is an amazing reality. I steal from you, but instead of you prosecuting me for committing that crime, you actually give me a wonderful, extremely costly gift with all your love in response to my being a thief!

That is certainly one for our finite, little minds to try to grasp; the King coming in love to the aid of the rebels when they need His help and assistance, and then welcoming them back into His kingdom as full citizens with no revenge or punishment given to them for the rebellion.

Yet He did give this Gift, and despite all I have and all I see around me, there is absolutely nothing for which I am more thankful. However, I do not want to personally be simply a "reservoir" to hold that Gift to myself. Instead I want to be an aqueduct used for that love to flow out abundantly through me to our whole world; a fountain of love that gives out as generously as is possible also.

That is the challenge we have before us as benefactors of His love, to make that love message more universal on a daily basis! So let us pick up the torch, and then run to our dark world with the wonderful light of His love message to them and for them. "This little light of mine" surely does need to shine into our very needy world today.

I stood guilty before the Judge, legally convicted of my many crimes, and I was rightfully sentenced to eternal death. But just imagine the shock and excitement on my part when the Judge who had just passed the sentence on me then reached down and offered me a "receipt" for the payment of the crimes I had committed, and it read cleanly; "Paid In Full!"

Suddenly, I am free to go and will never again have to face any further accusations from Him for any of my pardoned crimes. I am free at last with a total pardon, but also with an invitation from Him to become a much loved member of His royal family!

The Judge brought down a just guilty verdict and rightfully sentenced me to death as the price for my crimes, and then He offered me the "receipt" for full payment. It was a complete pardon for the crimes for which I was justly found legally guilty, but now the judgment and the resulting punishment rightfully assigned to me for my many crimes has been totally overwritten by a full pardon signed by His own blood. He paid it all Himself with the offering of Himself as the full payment! No wonder we are so very appreciative of that act of His giving of that Gift to cover us forever.

All I had to do was reach out and accept the receipt as full, total payment and then walk away debt free. Totally bankrupt and then instantly invited to become a member of a billionaire's family! It should not be all that difficult to be thankful that He gave, and I certainly suspect it is not, for I am one of the number one cheerleaders of His giving and also of His actual Gift!.

He had no other choice but to love, because not only does God actively love but God IS love; love in essence, and the personification of love in totality. That is the motivation behind the fact 'that He gave". An overflowing vessel just so easily and naturally gives and continues to give over and over again. And since there is an endless supply of His love, it continues to overflow and pour out to you, to me, and also to the whole world from that endless, limitless and unbounded supply. His love has no limit so we just continue to help ourselves to all we need and also to all we can give to our world as well!

That love we celebrate and revel in certainly was not a passive love in any way. It is most surely an extremely active love in every possible sense. In fact, as I write that word "passive" before the word "love" I am challenging myself as to whether these two words can actually be correctly placed together in the same sentence anyway. How can love possibly be considered "passive"; is any such thing as passive love even possible?

God's love surely was not passive, and is certainly not so even today either. It was an active love in creation, redemption and will continue to be so even into the eternal futures as well for us. And as they say, "we ain't seen nothin' yet"! The old hymn states it so correctly for us when it says that, "He giveth and giveth and giveth again". It just flows out continuously with no shutoff tap built into the supply system anywhere.

The first move was God's move. It was certainly not that we came to Him begging for forgiveness and for His help, and because He loved us He "bent the rules a little" and took us back. His love was, and still is, extremely aggressive. He gave to enable Him to reach us long before we made any effort to try to ever reach out to Him for help. "And I personally love You so much, Lord, for that very fact, for it has been by far the greatest influence in my whole life, and certainly will continue to be so for eternity."

Another amazing factor in trying to understand that giving is the fact that the Gift Himself was also in on the giving as well; the Son was part of that marvelous giving decision in eternity past! Sort of like Jesus Himself "taking off His own shirt" and then personally handing someone a lash for them to whip Him! The Father gave his Son, but the Son also gave Himself and we will zero in on that double-edged fact in the next chapter.

To a great extent the giving and the Gift are one and the same; God in three Persons, a blessed Trinity! So the God who gave and the God who was given are one in essence; a triune God! It is surely difficult to fully grasp this concept for sure but it is certainly a total reality nevertheless.

Love has no other choice other than to give. It is not self centered. Love certainly brings a sense of satisfaction to the "lover" himself, but it is primarily about, and focused upon its object. So He gave to cover us, so that from then onward whenever a holy God looks at us, He sees only the covering that He has given us, if we have simply reached out and accepted that covering for ourselves. Calvary certainly does cover it all as the old hymn so correctly states. Our past with all of its sin and all of its shame totally covered for us in that one basic act by Jesus on Calvary that memorable day.

God, as a "tri-unity", therefore reached inside His very heart and gave the very best Gift He could give. And nobody ever looking at that Gift since it was originally given, has ever been able to doubt the reality of His love for us. In fact, nobody has even been able to fully understand the magnitude and scope of that love of His for us either. Eternity will not be long enough for us to fully grasp its limits. "Limits" is probably not a good word here for how can there possibly be any limits to a limitless love?

In that act of providing redemption and reconciliation for us to Himself, He gave far more than all of His original creation combined; and in the process it cost Him a million times more to do so than the total creation could ever have cost Him in the beginning. It was truly a most wonderful, priceless Gift! It is a very interesting concept and such a beautiful picture to think of the Creator actually giving a Gift to vividly show and express His love for His most prized creation in the universe He had Himself created.

God and giving in the same sentence, which also includes us as the motivation and objective of that giving, makes for an extremely interesting picture indeed. He gave for certain; that is what Calvary was all about, and He gave because He loved us. God was giving us a Gift of love, and basically in the process saying to us, "I cannot give you something that will cost me nothing so I will bring you a Gift that will actually cost Me everything". No "bargain basement" gift purchasing here with God! No one ever looking at that Gift has ever been able to say to Him since it was given that day; "God, Your Gift was so very cheap!"

We are now ready to unwrap this Gift, and then clearly see just what it actually is. We certainly are going to be amazed when we do see just what that wonderful Gift actually is that He gave to us, because of His love affair with us, and then we will begin to understand a little more of the cost of that Gift once we do open it and actually "see" the Gift itself We will start to "unwrap" this Gift in the next chapter, and I am certain it will be another Thanksgiving for all of us once we actually see the Gift for ourselves!

Here then is the actual Gift! So Merry Christmas, Happy Birthday, Happy Easter, Happy New Year, Happy Thanksgiving, Happy Valentines Day and a whole lot more. It is all included there in this one wonderful Gift! And it certainly is the greatest Gift ever given by anyone to anyone for any occasion! Nothing more is ever needed to show us His love for the world.

"God, we now know for certain that You really do love us, and that it was not just "easy talk" on Your part when You told us that You loved us. You have proven it beyond any doubt with this Gift!"

CHAPTER 11

"HIS ONLY BEGOTTEN SON" THE SUPREME GIFT OF HIS LOVE

God is giving "His" Son, so the Gift is actually certainly His from the start, and now He is about to give this great Gift to us as well. So that personal Gift He gave to us was far more than something or someone from His original creation, or even from any subsequent creative act on His part. The Gift instead was part of the original Godhead/Creator Trinity who actually made it all at the very beginning of time. That is certainly an impressive Gift for sure. The Gift was not a mere creation; it was instead the Creator Himself!

The Gift was "His" because He is part of the Godhead, and so the Godhead reached inside itself and gave "His" only Son! I certainly realize that it is somewhat confusing for any of us to understand, that the Trinity actually reached inside itself and gave part of itself as the Gift of its combined love for all of us. Yet that is an actual reality just the same. It is surely mind boggling, but undeniably real at the very same time.

The very darling and crown jewel of heaven being given to us as the ultimate Gift of God's love for us is quite an amazing reality to grasp. The very object of angelic worship from the eons of eternity past, is suddenly wrapped in the body of a baby boy, and so very lovingly and quietly given to us as the Gift of the ages, and then placed in a bed of hay in a lonely barn in the town of Bethlehem. I can only imagine all of heaven watching very intently as He was gently dropped into that manger that night.

"He has gone", the angels must have said to each other that night He left heaven for Bethlehem! What a major event it must have been in heaven for sure, yet it went almost totally unnoticed at the time here on earth. This was the very first time heaven had been without Him as He was slipped so very quietly into a young woman's arms in a lowly stable, likely hidden somewhere in the back yard of that fully booked simple inn in Bethlehem.

Certainly even that inn itself was no five-star hotel, for a simple laborer from that time to have even tried to find a room there, but they found even that simple inn was full, and instead Joseph had to take his very pregnant wife out back to a barn for the night. And all heaven surely watched very closely as they settled into that crude shelter for that memorable night. Bethlehem surely became the central focus of all of heaven that night; from the Father to every angel there as well. All were certainly totally focused upon that stable that night.

God's only Son, invested by His Father to a recently married, young lady of very humble status, and to her new husband, who was a carpenter. God must have really trusted her for sure, and Joseph must also have been a very understanding young man to take the responsibility of raising a Child he knew was actually not his own Child, but he accepted the angel's message that the Child had been miraculously placed in Mary's womb by God Himself, and fully agreed to be the earthly father to raise that Child and work hard to provide for Him.

So they both must have fully believed the angel's messages to each of them, despite how completely impossible these messages must have first sounded to each of them at the time. A simple, peasant woman and a humble young "apprentice" carpenter, just setting up a tiny home for themselves, and trying to get a small carpentry business going for himself, then suddenly they have all of heaven's attention totally focused upon them.

From the worship and adoration of heaven's angelic hosts to the arms of a simple, yet specifically chosen, young lady named Mary. From the throne room of the universe to a manger in a stable; now there is a stepping down for certain. And then from that stable to a carpenter's humble home after leaving the mansions of heaven only to then have His parents told by angels to leave their simple home there and flee to Egypt for their lives, because Herod was aggressively looking for Him to kill Him.

So He became a child refugee right from the very start of His earthly life. A refugee from heaven to a manger and then having to be carried in mom's arms across the hot, dry Sinai desert for many days to a land where they likely knew nobody, and probably could not even speak the local language. From heaven to being a child refugee in Egypt to save His young life from the very start was certainly quite a stepping down for God's only Son.

From the golden streets of heaven later to the dusty roads, paths and trails of Canaan and Galilee and certainly having to walk them on foot Himself most of the time, likely in a simple pair of hand-made sandals. No fancy running shoes for Him for sure. From the "All Hails" of the angels around His throne, to the screams of, "Crucify Him" just thirty-three years later in Jerusalem. It was quite a stepping down for certain in the giving of this Gift.

He also went all the way from stretching out His hands to part the seas, to later willingly stretching them out this time to be cruelly spiked to a cross. When God gave His only Son, He sure did not hold back on that giving in any way! That is truly giving to the extreme for certain. But when God decided to give he held nothing back. He went all the way with it for sure.

So the first step in the giving of His only Son was to give Him to Mary. I have often wondered if she really understood who she was holding so tenderly in her motherly arms. Can you just imagine Mary looking into His tiny face and saying to Him as He lay there in her arms; "I love You so much". And His very presence there in her arms actually saying to her, and to the whole world as well, even without her hearing or fully understanding it at the time, "and I also love you so much as well, and that is why I have come. Mom, you will fully understand exactly what I mean some day."

I wonder how often she watched Him playing as a little child, and just sat there and looked at Him and wondered about His Father, the God of the universe, and what this whole mystery of her having a child was all about. Did she really realize she had been entrusted with raising the Son of the Creator right there in her so very humble home?

Even with her limited understanding of the significance of the plan of the ages that she was such a vital part of, I wonder how she felt about the task she had been entrusted with by God Himself, and about her very vital role in bringing it to reality.

"So please keep Him safe, Mary, for the eternal destinies for untold millions down through the centuries depend solely upon His actually living to be thirty-three years of age!"

The angel said to Mary, "You are to call His name Jesus, because He is going to save His people from their sins". So naturally that is what she called Him. But how could she ever have suspected that two thousand years later millions of people around the world that she did not even know existed in her time, because it had not even been discovered in her day, would still be singing, "Jesus is the sweetest name I know. And He is just the same as His lovely name. That's the reason why I love Him so, for Jesus is the sweetest name I know."

"Oh, Mary, if you could have only fully understood your role in God's eternal plan." She certainly knew He was so very special for sure, but did she really know just how special that would be?

I saw a short movie clip some time ago showing Mary cooking at her open fire just outside her simple little home, and Jesus as a boy of about six or seven years of age was coming running towards her as she worked. But as He was running down a couple of crude steps to get there to her, He stumbled and fell head first to the ground. Mary immediately dropped her pot and ran as fast as possible to Him to pick Him back up and to lovingly brush the dust from Him, and hugged Him closely to herself as a mother would naturally do. I wonder if she really did know who she was actually hugging so closely that day.

It is no wonder the song writer asked the question, "Mary, did you know?" Did she come close to grasping the actual reality of who He was as she took care of Him daily and watched Him grow? So He was given first to Mary, but He was also given so much further than simply to the home of a Jewish carpenter and his young bride. It was actually indeed so very much further than that, as we most certainly already know.

Not only was the Gift God's Son but the Gift was part of the giving God as well. That is mind boggling for certain. God actually giving God as a Gift to us to express God's love for us is quite a challenge for us to grasp. How do we get our minds around such an amazing reality?

But the Gift was nevertheless as much God Himself as the Father who gave Him was also God. So in one sense, it is God giving His Son and in another sense it is God giving Himself. If you are interested in taking on a real challenge, then just try to get your mind around that one and to grasp it.

It says "only", so the Gift is not only His Son, but is also the only one of its kind that God has; with none other like Him anywhere else in the whole universe, and Mary holds Him tightly in her arms. He was totally original and completely unique in Himself; God had none other. He was God's only Son and none other even came close to Him.

Yet His passionate love for us caused Him to become the "aggressor" in this whole redemption story, and also caused Him to give that only Son, knowing that He could never be replaced; returned to Him for certain, but never able to be replaced.

I wonder how much time God spent "searching" the towns around Bethlehem before He chose Mary to place within her virgin womb "His only Son"? I wonder also how He must have searched the same area looking for a future husband for Mary; a husband for her who would accept the situation, despite certainly being overwhelmed by the mind boggling realities for him personally. One who had some carpenter's skill, so that he could provide the very basics of life for this child of mystery given to him through his wife, Mary. A carpenter to work daily to get enough food to feed God's only Son a meal of rice or maize each day to prevent Him from being too hungry.

I wonder why God did not make sure there was a room empty in the inn that night that Mary and Joseph turned up there needing a place to rest. No computer hotel reservations guaranteed with your credit card for certain in those days; just on a walk-in basis only. There is not ever any indication that God even told Joseph to "step on it" that day as they traveled, to be sure he would get there before the hotel was fully booked.

But God did reserve a stable with a feeding manger and some dry hay for them to sleep on that night until Jesus arrived! No clean sheets; just the hay the animals had not yet eaten. I wonder if the Father stopped the animals from eating it all so His Son could have a bed that night! This was God taking care of His only Son as He was entrusted to Mary and Joseph that night. He simply reserved a stable for them!

It must have been quite a challenge for the Father to have placed His only Son there in that stable that night, and also to hand Him over to that poor Jewish couple. But, of course, we all know that was just the easy part of the actual process in relationship to this giving of His only Son to us that day. The cost to God for the Bethlehem aspect of the giving of His Son was only the down payment on the whole process. The much bigger cost of that giving of that Gift was billed to heaven about 33 years later!

The hymn poses this challenging situation to us when it says, "Just suppose God searched through heaven, and could not find one willing to be, the supreme sacrifice that was needed to bring eternal life to you and me." But I am so thankful He did find One willing to be that sacrifice for me, and that One was His only Son and by mutual agreement He came! There was no hesitation, no holding back in any way on His part. It was a total acceptance of the challenge and a complete commitment on His part to fulfilling it.

Then the full bill for the real total cost of the redemption transaction arrived in heaven from Jerusalem. God's Son in the person of Jesus, lying on His back on two pieces of rough, likely already bloodstained timber from previous crucifixions, which had been carved from a tree His Father had so intentionally planted on a Jewish hillside years before, cut down and nailed or tied together to hold a human body with His arms outstretched in both directions, and used over and over again to get rid of the most "undesirables" of their society at that time.

And now it is God's only Son's time to lie there, stretch out His arms, and be so cruelly and painfully attached there likely with rusty, secondhand spikes to hold Him to that cross. But it was certainly not these nails that actually kept Him on the cross that day. It was instead the previously stated, amazing fact that God so loved all of us, that He just had no other choice other than to die for us to bring us back once again to Himself by that very painful act, and how we surely need to keep praising Him for that fact.

So a state employee came along with a hammer and some nails and held one of the Son's hands securely on the wood, probably kneeling on His arm so that both of his own hands would be free to hold the hammer and the nails. He then started the process God had planned for giving us a gift to express His love that was certainly well worthy of its source.

He nailed Jesus to that cross, and then dropped the cross with a terrible jolt into the hole in the ground to make the hanging there even more painful for Him as He died. This is what our sins first of all, but also God's love for us despite our sins, brought to Jesus that day. I was actually one of the most painful deaths possible for anyone to die.

God had only one Son, and yet He gave Him that day to Calvary to die for us, because He loved us so much. That most certainly must have been quite a love affair, and quite a painful gift as well for both the Father and the Son, and also for Mary as she watched this Son of promise die in such agony, totally rejected by the religious leaders, and not having been given the chance to be the Messiah she had expected Him to become!

Can you just imagine her secret questioning of what she was seeing happening there that day on Calvary? "Now what; what went wrong? Surely this is not why God gave me His Son!"

I have also wondered if that "hammer man" knew how special he himself was that day, and what a significant role he was actually playing in history and also for eternity, but I certainly doubt that he did. He nailed six hands to crosses that day and to him the hands of a carpenter's Son and the hands of thieves all look very much alike.

Not even the shrewdest of judges can simply look at a man's hands and know if he is guilty and deserving death or not! He was playing the most vital role in the whole of human history there that day, and yet he simply thought it was just another day's dirty job and no more! I wonder if he even told his family when he got home that night about what he had done that day.

It actually makes me want to apologize to Him for what they did to Him there on Calvary that day, until I then realize afresh that it was all part of the Father's giving plan of His only Son, to thereby enable Him to then bring many sons and daughters to glory through His sacrifice that day.

As a consequence of God's giving there that day, the central attraction of heaven from eternity has now become the central attraction for millions of worshippers on a daily basis throughout the whole world as well! And there is certainly no doubting the actual fact that this was really God's original intent right from the very start anyway. He wanted to turn rebels into worshippers and so He willingly set up the process to make that contrast possible.

"Begotten Son". Please do not expect me to explain that one as it relates to the Trinity! Three in one; all eternal with no beginning or ending and yet one called the "only Begotten Son". That relationship will take eternity for me to get my mind around unless God has plans to put a whole lot more brains in my head on that day when I finally get home than what I now have there at present and I surely hope He does!

Begotten? You ask God yourself when you get to heaven about that relationship, and when He explains it to you and you fully understand it, then you come over near His throne, and you will certainly find me at that time. Then you can tell me the answer as well! Is that okay with you?

Or does the word "begotten" refer instead to that simple stable birth; the only member of the Godhead to be born and have a human body that needed care as a baby; feeding in Mary's arms, being bathed daily in his mother's tiny container of water, tucked cozily into a crude little bed that His foster father, Joseph, had carefully made for Him to sleep snugly in through the night? You choose for yourself on that one. But one thing we do know for certain, and that is the fact the Gift was His only begotten Son!

God gave His Son. There is no indication He asked for any angel to volunteer to be that gift to us. He simply stayed "right inside the divine family" to find the One to send and I stand so amazed by that reality! God certainly owed us nothing whatsoever, yet He gave us everything nevertheless. No wonder we fall on our faces in love and appreciation to Him, and then rise to serve Him so passionately ourselves. What else would anyone expect us to do in the face of such amazing love as he has shown to us?

His Son; there with the Father from all eternity past as the Father's pride, joy and constant companion, coming to begin to live a very simple life in a Roman occupied Jewish town in tiny Israel, but certainly coming with a very specific mission at the center of His program for His time here as well. He had been present there in heaven when that decision had been made to form Adam out of the dust of the earth and Eve from Adam's side. (Read Proverbs 8:22-31 for a slight glimpse of this wonderful reality of His eternal existence with the Father.)

He was there when the decision was made to give them reproductive capabilities, and there also when the decision was made to give them the free will, and the right to choose to serve their Creator or to willfully sin against Him. There, knowing from the start that the right to have a free will would some day cause nails to have to be driven in His own hands and feet, and yet fully supporting the decision to create Eden and place a couple within it with free wills and reproductive capacities. So the giving of the Son started long before Mary's day! It stretched back even before Eden actually became a reality.

Then many centuries later He gave that "only" Son to this young Jewish virgin; who had just married a carpenter. My father was also a carpenter all his working life and he always found it interesting that Jesus as a child probably did some carpenter work Himself to help his "foster father" there in Nazareth. He was also quite fascinated by the fact that God chose a carpenter to provide for Jesus while He was a child! Dad always felt it was quite an honor for him to be doing that same job himself.

God gave His only Son and "only" when it refers to God is pretty unique. You can only barely begin to imagine that love relationship within the

Godhead. Nothing can come close to illustrating it, so just let your own imaginations run wild. And then I read of a conclusion made by that Godhead that is simply a part of a conversation between Them in the throne room as together They simply decided to make man in Their very own image. They knew the cost before the decision was ever made, yet the decision was unanimous anyway.

So that "decision" was made there with full knowledge of the fact that it would mean that one day one of the members of the Godhead would have to endure spikes being driven through His hands and feet because of what they together decided to do. What a consequence for the Godhead to have to face as a result of such a decision. On that basis the "Gift" was given then and there, and from there onward the donor never once regretted that decision so He willingly gave the Gift! He "kissed a guilty world in love" and then gave us His only one of a kind very special Gift.

What is "the world" worth in God's eyes? That is quite a challenging question to try to answer until you look at the Gift He gave to bring that world back into a renewed loving relationship with Himself. That Gift was certainly all He could "afford" and then some; it was really quite a Gift for sure! Yet He originally owned it all, and as we also know, that certainly included us as well as the very top product from His creative hands.

Calvary was certainly not any surprise to God, nor was it an emergency response to our terrible rebellion to try to fix something that had not gone according to His original plan. He already knew the cost when He said at the very beginning, "Let's make them just like us"!

The introduction of the slaying of an innocent lamb on an altar after Eden's rebellion was not an attempt to try to fix the problem. God knew right from the start these lambs would not work for us just there on their own, to bring the forgiveness we all so desperately needed. They were accepted simply as "promissory notes" of "full payment" being made in the future. God accepted the lamb with the understanding He would send the real Lamb who would certainly Himself at that time then have the capability to cover all the debt with His life being given on a Roman cross.

I see God looking down from heaven upon every lamb that was even slaughtered upon an altar from Eden to Calvary and saying to His Son; "That is You when the time is right!" What it must have cost God even before Bethlehem or Calvary to watch the foreshadowing of His Son dying for us on a cross with every lamb that was offered.

That giving of His only Son as a Gift to cover that guilty verdict upon the whole race, and to totally pay the penalty that verdict demanded, was not simply a one-time action that was over with in three days, or even took a whole thirty-three years to complete. It was a Gift made with every sacrifice accepted upon man-made altars through the centuries prior to Calvary, because it foreshadowed the shameful, agonizing death Jesus would one day face on that Roman cross on that time-splitting, historical day!

But from Calvary onward, no more lambs would need to die upon altars, for the Lamb to which all previously slain lambs had pointed had now Himself been offered once and for all time. Once that full payment was made by His Son then no further foreshadowing of that payment would ever be needed to be made upon any Jewish altar.

In Genesis 22:2 God told Abraham to go into the hills to offer a sacrifice, but for him not to take any lamb for the altar. Instead his only legitimate son, Isaac, was to be placed on the altar. What a picture! Except that in this case the son, Isaac, was not aware of the plan, so he asked his father about the absence of any lamb for the sacrifice and Abraham responded, "My son, God Himself will provide Himself a sacrifice!"

I have often marveled at how long-term that response to Isaac by Abraham proved to be. God Himself provides Himself as the sacrifice! What a tremendous foreshadowing of Calvary that statement was, for that is exactly what God did there that day on that cross on Mount Calvary. He gave Himself as the Sacrifice when He actually gave His Son to die for us.

He keeps giving that Gift to every sinner who bows before Him for forgiveness for his transgression. No wonder the hymn writer wrote that, "out of His infinite riches in Jesus, He giveth and giveth and giveth again." Calvary certainly does cover it all, and His giving there that day has proven effective ever since the day that cruel cross held His only Son upon it to die there for us. God provided the sacrifice, and none other has ever been required since He did so that day two thousand years ago.

I am amazed on a daily basis when I think of the fact that God loves me. I am also amazed by the reality that He loved me despite the fact I was unlovable, and would personally require so much work done in me for certain for a holy God to bring me into His family, and into His Home to stay.

I stand in total awe when I realize that He fully knew that it would cost Him His only Son to continue that love affair with me, yet He lovingly proceeded down that actual road anyway, totally undaunted by the tremendous cost involved in His doing so. The cost was quite minor in God's thinking compared to what He received back as a result of that Gift He gave to us that day.

We are called "children of God" but it is only Jesus to which God refers as "His only begotten Son". I am thrilled to be a son of God, but when I see the word "only" before "Son" in relationship to Jesus I am in no way confused. In fact, I am overjoyed with the fact that my "adoption papers" into the family of the eternal God were signed and sealed with the very blood of His "only" Son! That makes for quite a secure "signature" to bring me into His family, and I have placed my total trust solely in it.

"His" only Son for certain, but He was so very willing to share His only Son with us. There is nothing selfish for sure in the word His in this verse, especially when it is preceded by the words "He gave". Nor is there anything exclusive or in any way closing any doors to us in the use of that word "only". If God loved me enough to allow His only Son to be crucified for me, then that is a good enough love affair for me to respond to, and also return it to its source with all the passion I have. I am so very thankful to have been personally redeemed by His only Son, and consequently to have been adopted into His very family.

I have often tried to imagine how this decision was originally made that began this whole process of redemption. I fully realize that trying to understand the inner workings of the eternal Godhead is futile but I still like to imagine it anyway. Did the Father ask His Son if He would be willing to go to earth and to die upon a cross, if they gave man a free will before even creating Adam, and the right to choose between serving God, or instead rebelling against their Creator? Or did the Son Himself ask the Father if He could be the one who would go and die to pay the penalty for that rebellion? It was certainly such a costly decision made by such a loving God for such a rebellious world!

Was there ever any "discussion" as to whether fallen angels should also be given the option to be included in the "whosoever"? Did any still loyal angel volunteer to take the Son's place on that future Roman cross? Was it the Father's decision alone or was it a joint decision of the Godhead. God had only one Son and He gave Him and I strongly suspect it was a unanimous decision of the Trinity, because the love affair with us comes equally from each of the "three in one" to us.

He gave His only Son and we need to shout that message loud and clear to our sinful, needy world that the King of the universe has now become part of our race; just like us in every way except without sin, and we know that in God's thinking the death of His innocent Son covered the sin of our whole guilty race! We have been given a second chance, with a totally clean record, and no 'past balances" to be settled before we are "debt free".

CHAPTER 12

"THAT WHOSOEVER" THE BROAD SCOPE OF HIS LOVE

❧

"Whosoever" is certainly a very all inclusive word as it is used here in this verse. It certainly means anyone for it is, as just stated, an all inclusive word for sure, and yet at the very same time it is also a conditional word as well. Whosoever actually does not force anything on anyone at all! Instead it offers the total package to anyone who wants it and then personally makes the decision to accept it.

"Whosoever" is not specifically about anybody, until they have individually met the requirements to qualify for inclusion, and have then accepted its provision for themselves. It is only then inclusive of everyone who does do so. Therefore whosoever does require a personal response from everyone who wants to be included in its scope! Yet the response required to be included is extremely simple to understand and then follow.

So actually whosoever is not simply a passive, all inclusive word, nor is it a "whether you want it or not, you have it" word. Instead it has a very strong "if you want it, you have it" concept included in it. So it is not a "just sit back and wait for it to happen" idea. Whosoever is everybody but with a qualifier, so it really then becomes anybody who…..! It is "a make sure you are included in it yourself" word. So grab it for yourself and be sure!

If anyone wants in on "whosoever" then they are most welcome, but they do have a part to play themselves to make it happen for them personally in order to be certain they are included in its scope. Thankfully the role we personally have to play to ensure our own inclusion in all of the assured benefits that follow is quit a simple, basic one that anyone and everyone can so easily follow, and can comply fully with at any time they wish to do so.

Yet this fact of needing a personal action for inclusion has absolutely nothing to do with our personal "earning" of anything whatsoever from God by ourselves. Instead, it simply involves personally accepting what God has already done for us on an individual, personal basis. I did not pay the "fine" for my sins; I just accepted the receipt for the payment He already made, and will certainly use that "receipt" as my entrance "ticket" into eternal life and heaven. And "whosoever" can have a personal copy of that "receipt: for themselves as well. It is just that simple to be included!

So there then is the guarantee of total inclusion, and also of free admissions for me, because He paid the cost and I simply accepted that receipt for myself. That receipt is also universally available, for it is for the "whosoever". Simply reach out and take it personally for yourself, and then point others towards it with full assurance of its availability to them as well!

I am reminded of the old chorus that I use to hear at church when I was young. It went like this; "Whosoever surely meaneth me, surely meaneth me, surely meaneth me. Whosoever surely meaneth me; whosoever meaneth me!" Pretty basic truth there that I am included in this whosoever, but it surely is a truth well worth repeating. It is all inclusive for certain, yet nevertheless only for those who want personally to be included in that great offer from God.

God certainly does not exclude anyone from its scope Himself, but we can actually exclude ourselves either willfully, by saying no thank you to the receipt, or so very sadly, being excluded because for whatever reason we never heard of the payment having been made for us, and therefore could not respond to the invitation, nor accept it personally for ourselves simply because tragically, we did not hear of or know about its availability to us.

So we are included in that whosoever, unless we personally choose to exclude ourselves either actively or passively from its scope. If you want into God's family, and have asked for that inclusion there, then I am delighted to have you as part of my eternal family as well, because I am certain that I am personally in on that offer myself, and I surely intend to stay right there.

None of any of the sins of our past will exclude any one of us from the benefits we are about to read about, unless we do not accept His offer for ourselves. The price for the sins of our past has already been fully paid. But we each need that receipt for the payment to actually cover us, and He offers us here the invitation to come get it from Him for ourselves and get it absolutely free as well.

Do you see your name written clearly on that invitation to pick up the receipt? I saw mine many years ago and "grabbed" it, and have securely kept it in the "security chest" of my heart to this day!

So "whosoever" is you if you choose inclusion, and "whosoever" is also me because I have certainly already done so for myself. Our heavenly Host says "whosoever" can be part of the bride, and who would ever be crazy enough to refuse to accept such a wonderful proposal and invitation! It should be irresistible from that very positive perspective for sure, but certainly even more so when we look at the extremely negative alternative to accepting the offer from God which is presented here in this verse.

I am part of the whosoever because I desperately need to be included for my eternal protection, but also because I actually want that personal inclusion for the wonderful, positive benefits assured me there for eternity as well. I have personally gone for inclusion for both negative as well as positive reasons, and we will deal with both of these in the last two chapters of this section.

But the yet unanswered question here is actually "whosoever what?" Everything in this whole verse up to this point has been totally God-centered. Now we are about to be faced with what we have to do ourselves to take full advantage of everything previously shown us, from God's love for us to the action He undertook to cover us with the benefits of that love.

But now "whosoever" demands some affirmative action from each of us individually in order for us to be included in these benefits of God's love, including His personally acting upon that passionate love that He has clearly stated He has for us. So the question for us remains basically, whosoever what? And that for certain is the really key, crucial question we need to examine. What is God looking for from us to ensure we are back in His family which our original parents left in Eden?

You can only imagine the possibilities here for an answer from God. "Lord, what do I have to do to be included in the benefits of what you did for us"? Can you imagine the tenseness of waiting for the reply to that question? Just think what He could have said! He could easily have set requirements that were practically impossible for us to ever meet ourselves. Then what would our plight have been had He done so?

CHAPTER 13

"Believeth in Him" The Liberating Message of His Love

Instead of some extremely demanding requirements being set for anyone to be included in the benefits, John simply added; "believeth in Him". We stop, and we wait anxiously for any additional required actions on our part to be added to this simple act of believing, but then we realize there actually are no more. That is it; believing in Him is the only requirement. Nothing else demanded, required or even suggested. Simply believe in Him, and we are immediately in on the total benefits that Calvary's sacrifice has made available to our world.

Believe, and heaven's gates will open wide for us when we stand before them. Believe, and our slate will be wiped clean and even the dust shaken from the eraser. Believe, and all our past records are immediately destroyed forever. They are cast into the sea of God's forgetfulness, wherever that might be, and as the song states, there is a "No

Fishing!" sign posted there on the shoreline as well, so don't anyone try to "fish" them out on us.

I am personally so very glad there is no "instant replay" on God's forgiveness records. And certainly no save option on His "computer" records of a believer's past, prior to his believing. Believing deletes the previous records with no recovery of deleted info option available even to God, or to anyone else either who may wish to dig into our forgiven past at any time even for all of eternity. Believe in Him and that is all that is required to start all over again!

Believing in someone can be easy, or it can be almost impossible; it just depends on whom it is that you are expected to put your trust. So how about believing in Him? Does that sound difficult or perhaps even a dangerous thing to do? You must remember that the "Him" has previously been identified as God's only Son. That amazing fact should certainly make the believing in Him so much easier.

If we are going to believe in anyone, or anything for that matter, what better target could there possibly be for our believing to be placed in than the Creator/God of everything that we can see around us? Sure sounds to me like a reliable target for our believing to be focused upon.

He is the expert! He was there in the beginning when the very first couple was made. In fact, He actually made them both Himself. Our finding it difficult to believe in Him for help, or not trusting Him to be able to do so because we do not think He knows what He is doing, is far worse that saying Henry Ford knew nothing about cars.

What does God know about eternity? What did Ford know about "internal combustion engines"? Well for a start, Ford likely invented them himself anyway. So that should certainly qualify him as having a fair amount of knowledge on the subject. But what does God know about us anyway, and can we actually trust Him to have the most complete knowledge available on His creation? I certainly do think we can.

So how about this "Him" that we are told here to believe in and totally trust? Does He come close to having the kind of eternal knowledge and experience needed when it comes to being a reliable source to put our trust in, and to also believe fully in Him at all times?

Two thieves died with Jesus on Calvary that day He died. You can read the actual account of these two thieves dying beside Jesus that day on Calvary in Luke 23: 39-43. It shows us how one simply "believed" in Him, even in its simplest form, but the other one did not believe in Him, and the critical difference it made for the believing thief.

In fact, these two "buddies in crime" never saw each other again after that day! They both went in two very different directions to two very different eternal destinations from there. That is what believing "in Him" will do. That believing in Him is just so simple, and so very basic that a criminal in terrible pain, hanging on a cross was able to do so despite the distractions of his pain and actually dying in such agony.

Just look for a moment at these two thieves with Jesus on the crosses there that day on Calvary. Both were equally guilty, and I am certain also equally sinful, but they are today in two very different places for eternity for certain. Of course we recognize that it was Jesus who made the difference for that one thief, but what did that thief actually do to qualify him there that day for such a dramatic and sudden change in his destiny?

There was no sermon or altar call there on Calvary that day for certain. No praying a sinner's prayer; not even much evidence of repentance. Yet there certainly were a few interesting factors involved there on Calvary nevertheless. First he called Jesus, "Lord". There certainly was not much evidence at Mount Calvary on that day to confirm that for him, but he said it anyway. So he recognized divinity even when it was being crucified right beside him there on Calvary that day.

He must have also believed there was life after the death they were all three dying, because he specifically asked to be remembered at a further point in Jesus' future. He also must have felt that this man on the middle cross was someone very special, because he actually talked about Him having a future kingdom. So he said, "Some day in the future just take a moment and remember me", and Jesus then replied to him, "I can certainly do much better than that for you. In fact, today you will actually be with me in Paradise!" Such a simple act of "believing in Him", yet it produced such spectacular, instant but also eternal results for that dying thief that very day!

Such spectacular results can come by simply believing, and then acting upon that very belief. I doubt very much that dying thief expected the results of that very basic act of believing on his part in the One dying beside him to be so rapid, nor anywhere near as amazing for him as it actually turned out to be. But his believing in Him certainly made it happen for him. He tried it, and I am sure he liked it! And it sure beat the other alternative that his friend had to face later that day when he also died.

"Believing", even in its simplest form, changed eternity for that thief in a miraculous way. There is certainly nothing debatable on that one for sure. From perishing to eternal life instantly! That is surely what I would classify as a fast acting cure for a serious problem for certain. And there is definitely no false advertising in that statement for sure either. The results are fully guaranteed just as "advertised" for everyone.

I once asked a congregation if they had ever thought about how fortunate that guy was that he actually was a thief, and that he had been caught, found guilty and then sentenced to death by crucifixion on the very day and the very same hill on which Jesus was also crucified. Not much to feel fortunate about here so far, until you then realize that this is where he met the Savior, dying on that cross next to him that day, and then suddenly everything changed dramatically for him for eternity! How is that for our fast acting, as well as a long term cure that we can now offer to our world for its very serious potential eternal problems?

So believe in Him and act upon it. It is just that simple. If you do not believe you will not take any such action. Let me show you a very "complicated illustration" of that sequence of first believing and then acting upon what you believe, and you had better be ready to do some rather deep thinking on this one!

I sit in a car with an ignition key in my hand and I really struggle to "believe" that simply inserting that key in the little hole in front of me and giving it one turn to the right is all that is needed for that car to take me home. Of course there is no way that could ever work! How can it work; it is just too simple to be believable, so how could it possibly be true? So I take no action and I just sit there going nowhere because I cannot believe that anything that simple could produce such amazing results.

So does anyone have any suggestions for me as I sit there in my car with the key in my hand and I just wait, with my lack of faith in that key simply being inserted in that little hole and then turned getting me absolutely nowhere? Did I hear someone say, "Just believe it and put the key in the ignition and turn it? Do it and you will be amazed at the results if you do so."

So I try it, and now I am driving along and headed home! Who could have imagined that such a simple act of believing and then acting on that belief could produce such amazing results?

When I get to my heavenly home, I will surely be so happy I did believe in that "key" as well, and then acted upon that belief. (Have I lost you here yet with that one?) "Whosoever" puts the key in the ignition and turns it will start the car, and the car will then take them home. It actually works if you believe it, and then simply try it for yourself. Believing in Jesus will take you home even if you do not have a personal driver's license.

"Whosoever" has that amazing characteristic of having an extremely inclusion potential for everyone but "whosoever" also has a qualifier for inclusion for everyone as well, and that qualifier requires knowledge of the process for inclusion, and then personal action to be taken on that revelation of the action required. It is whosoever "believes in Him". That is certainly quite an easy qualifier for anyone for sure.

Note that the qualifier is to believe "in" Him and not simply to believe about Him. There is quite a difference in the two. Even most Muslims and also many non-Christians believe many or most things about Jesus, yet they certainly do not believe in Him. Yet believing "in Him" should not be so very difficult for anyone once they really do believe about Him!

In fact, if I believed the stories about Superman, then I might even believe in him, but fortunately I do not believe about him so therefore I simply do not believe in him either. So I am not actually quite as naïve as some people may think I am!

Yet I do believe the story about Jesus as God's Son dying for me on Calvary, then being raised from the dead the third day, and later taken up into heaven to await my coming there to meet Him, so therefore I also find it quite easy to "believe in Him" myself as well.

He is the God who, as part of the Creator Godhead, willingly stepped into His rebellious, fallen creation out of pure love, thereby to restore a broken relationship between Himself and His creation. So His motivations for presenting Himself to us and saying simply "believe in me" are above reproach. There are no false claims, promises or expectations whatsoever involved in this process. It is genuine and one hundred percent guaranteed one hundred percent of the time for anyone and everyone who chooses to take advantage of the offer.

Then He died; not by sickness or accident, but put to death by crucifixion with two guilty thieves, and yet He still took no action to prevent it from happening to Him that day. He knew that His dying was a most vital role for Him in making it possible for us to actually be able to "believe in Him", and then for us to see the actual results in our lives for eternity.

So He was put to death, and hundreds saw Him die on that dark day. His dead, multi-pierced, blood-stained body was taken from the cross, washed by a man named Joseph, wrapped in grave clothes, and then placed in Joseph's own private tomb. He was dead, gone, and it was over!

The entrance was then sealed, and guards placed by the authorities at the entrance for security for the dead body lest someone should try to steal it and make some insane, false claims about an actual resurrection, or some other such crazy, ridiculous story!

But despite all the precautions against thievery or possible fraud, and also the harsh reality that He was actually declared legally dead by the authority at the execution before being placed in the tomb, He was later seen by two men on the road to Emmaus and actually walked and talked with them for a while and even ate with them. Then he was seen by Peter, Thomas and the other disciple fully alive. Later He appeared to about five hundred at the same time and location!

Daily it was becoming easier to believe in Him. Proof was mounting continuously that death could not and had not held Him for any extended period of time. Three days and it was over; death had lost its evil grip on Him, and the believing in Him became such an easy exercise for anyone.

It may be easy to say it was all a conspiracy on their part to pretend He was alive again. But note this fact, and it is one that very few pay much attention to in relationship to the reliability of their story. But practically all the original disciples except John were executed for what they were claiming about a literal resurrection, and having seen Him alive, and many of the others who saw Him after His resurrection also died for actually claiming He was alive again, and yet not one of them ever recanted and admitted the story was fabricated.

If any one of them had "confessed" to fraud in the resurrection story, they surely would have been spared their executions, and then shown off by the religious leaders of the time as a "prime witness" against the early church's "fraudulent" claim of a literal resurrection and actual appearances of the crucified Jesus! But no such witness, who had previously seen Him alive, ever appeared on the scene making that claim. They all stuck with their story and many of them died for doing so! Does anyone think they would have willingly died for a lie, if they could have confessed to fraud and been spared for doing so?

The fact that the early church stuck to its claims of a literal resurrection for Jesus and His actual appearance to them in person is pretty difficult to refute. How is it possible to believe in someone who died by execution over two thousand years ago? The answer is quite simple; the story simply does not end there. In fact that is only the beginning of the epic recounting of the next amazing historical reality, for He has continued to transform lives since that day!

So believe, trust, rely in, depend upon and put your faith in Him. Hundreds of millions over the last twenty centuries have chosen to do so, and not one has ever been known to say, "I was promised something here but when I did what was required, I did not get what I was promised!" There have been no claims of "false advertising" ever laid against this verse and then proven to be a correct accusation. Obviously, it worked one hundred percent and nobody has ever had to "claim a refund" because it did not work as promised.

While the believing is important, yet it is the object of that believing that is the crucial factor; it is the believing in "Him". And I certainly cannot even imagine anyone better to put my trust in than Him. If I were looking for someone I could put my trust in to fly a plane for me, I would certainly go looking for a well experienced pilot. One of those "been there, done that" guys! That should not be too difficult to understand.

So when John says to believe "in Him" if you want the most reliable protection for your life here, and especially for eternity, it should not be any surprise that John is here referring to Jesus. He is "experienced" from all eternity. He is for certain the original "been there and done that" Person, for He has been there from all eternity! (John 1: 1-5)

Actually my believing in Him puts me securely in Him, so not only is my "believing" in Him but my "life" is actually also in Him as well. It is "hid with Christ in God" and that is security enough for me. Do you remember the old hymn, "The Haven of Rest"? One of the lines from that beautiful hymn says, "Now in Jesus I am safe ever more". That is taking the "believing in Him" to a new level of security of actually "being in Him"! In Him is security, peace, joy, fulfillment for both time and eternity. That is quite an offer.

So moving from believing to actually being in Him, which is the natural sequence in this process brings protection to us from the negatives, but it also brings inclusion in all of the positives as well. Next chapter we will examine the protection from the negatives this believing in Him brings, and then move from the negatives to the active positives that are consequently ours for the asking.

CHAPTER 14

"Should Not Perish" The Wonderful Protection of His Love

"For God so loved the world that he gave His only begotten Son that whosoever believeth in him SHOULD NOT PERISH" "Perish" is such a terrible word in any situation, but when it is applied to an eternal soul, and the perishing referred to is also an eternal situation, it certainly presents to us a tragedy beyond any description. It consequently becomes an extremely bleak, desperately dark picture for certain for anyone falling victim to this tragic, eternal state, which was certainly originally designed to securely hold Satan and his fallen angels only, and thereby prevent him from ever getting access to us ever again.

I am certainly so glad there is such a strong negative as "not' in the center of that three-word expression, and that it is then followed by a four-word extremely positive alternative. Without Calvary, only "perishing" would be possible for us, but because of that historic event on that mount that day, the negative "not" has now confidently placed before that dreadful word "perish", to assure us of His eternal protection for us. "So thank You, God, so very much for Calvary and for the protection it provided for us!"

Because of Calvary, John is now able to refer to "perishing" with that strong negative word "not" confidently placed before it for anyone willing to "believe in Him", yet tragically the very presence of that negative word "perish" in that expression, "should not perish" shows us that there is another side possible to this "perishing" possibility as well. And certainly that very negative potential that is present there, if you simply removed that word "not" from the phrase, is one that must be avoided by us at any cost.

I am so glad to report that God also looked at it in that same way Himself as well. That at any cost He had to make an escape route possible for us, so that His masterpiece in all of creation need not end up so perishing. Providing that escape route is what this verse has been all about. Therefore the resulting message now for us is that none need perish, if they simply choose His provided solution to the problem that actually made such perishing its most certain, assured consequence for us in the beginning.

God knew for certain that any possibility of our eventually perishing should be avoided at any cost so He paid the cost Himself to make that escape possible for anyone interested. To be eternally in a state here described in such a negative context as perishing is certainly not a very attractive picture.

But God loved us so much He had to make an escape from that potential situation available to us, and as we all know for sure, it was an escape "from" as well as an escape "to" that He then provided. However He did not include Satan in the escape for certain. Fortunately, no such alternative was offered to him, or to any of his evil cohorts, so he will be gone forever.

If believing in Him provides eternal protection from perishing, then it is only logical for us to assume that the lack of that believing will continue to lead to perishing in any individual who neglects to take full advantage of that alternative offer from God presented in this verse. Therefore an immediate positive response to that special invitation to believe in that escape route is absolutely imperative for us all individually.

So, whatever that future, eternal state of those who are still outside salvation's protection will be, it is here described as eternal perishing. What a desperate state that must be; perishing for certain, but then perishing forever. That is one very dark reality for anyone to have to face, or for us to even have to imagine for anyone for eternity. It is especially desolate when we realize the fact that it was not necessary for it to be so, had the lost heard and then simply "believed in Him". What a difference that would have made for them!

No one has to be forever separated from God, and eternally beyond and outside the reach of His love, but that is the only other alternative introduced from this perspective here in "should not perish". Instead of enjoying the protection of God's love, alternately to be continuously for eternity in the presence of Satan, and the total evil which always surrounds him.

In fact, even the word perish is far too good a word to describe such an eternal existence with Satan, because it will be an unending existence, whereas "perish" may actually leave some suggestion of termination in our minds. No such termination is here included in the word perish. It is instead an eternal existence in a state of "perishing"!

Little wonder we sing the challenge to "Rescue the Perishing" by sharing with them the message to simply believe in Him, and flashing out that message to the world from the lighthouse in the midst of the present storm. His radiant love for us all caused Him to raise the total ransom for all of us, and in so doing turned on the light of hope for the world to shine out from the lighthouses over these stormy seas for anyone, and for everyone caught in the storm to see, and then head immediately towards that light for eternal shelter and total safety.

I am so thankful that this word "not" actually does precede the word perish when it follows the concept of our simply believing in Jesus! So the first benefit presented by John here for that simple act of believing in Jesus is a major protection from an equally major potential negative; that anyone who does so should definitely not perish. Obviously nobody should have to perish, but it is equally obvious that some will actually do so, if they do not run to the shelter He provided in love by His sacrifice on Calvary.

Please excuse my language for a minute. But I really need to get a point across here for us to see. Have you ever heard anyone say angrily to another person, "Go to Hell"? I am sure we have all heard it said, perhaps even to us personally many times. I hear it, and I seriously wonder; "How could anyone hate another person enough that they would actually want them to go to hell?" Do we have any idea what that will be like for anyone who actually does go there? It certainly is not a pretty picture as we often say!

I am going to shock you here with this one. Actually, I personally feel sorry even for Hitler and Idi Amin and other such characters if that is where they went. I simply cannot wish for anyone to end up eternally perishing no matter how evil they may have been while they were living. So it is no wonder I am so concerned about the millions who have never heard of the other alternative whatsoever, and therefore know nothing about the simple, yet so very effective "escape route" that God has provided for them through Calvary.

Nobody, except Satan and his fallen angels ever deserve to end up there, but by neglecting the remedy that Calvary provided, many will find themselves in that same place as Satan with no way to escape. Trapped forever with Satan is certainly not a very pretty picture for sure. Personally I surely want to be as far away from Satan and his followers in that original rebellion as is possible for me to be for eternity.

Consequently I certainly have no intention of spending my eternity with him in the place God intended only for Satan and these fallen angels, better known as demons! He has already been far too much of a nuisance to me here now, but to be around him for eternity; not a chance! Good riddance is what I say regarding Him. I have no intention of spending any more time anywhere where Satan is allowed than what I have to do so here in this present life. "Just "scat" to where you belong, Satan, and stay there forever!"

The whole of the universal church, and that also includes every Christian in the church as well, needs to proclaim far and wide that none ever need perish. There is only one solution and only one sure escape from that very terrible possibility for anyone, and this escape route is very capable of handling all those who run to it for safety! And we know where that one escape route actually is for all of them. So it is such an easy, also an exciting task we have been given by the Provider Himself, and one that is guaranteed one hundred percent effective for now, and especially for eternity; simply believe in Him and anyone is covered.

Nobody should ever perish for certainly no one needs to have to face that reality. The provision is one hundred percent inclusive, and also the same percentage in effectiveness. Why drown, when the lifeboat is right there beside you, and the lifeline is being thrown out for anyone to grab hold of it, and then be quickly pulled to safety? So we go passionately after the perishing with everything we have, before they actually do perish, for then it will be eternally too late to help. Tragically, once someone does drown the lifeboat is then no longer of any assistance in bringing help to them.

Since there is a wide open door available to everyone, then why should anyone have to stand in a burning house and wait for the flames to consume them? So again, nobody should have to perish when the provision is so effective, and also so easily applied to our individual lives. If we take advantage of the provided protection, then we will not have to suffer the consequences of that original rebellion against God, and His rightful authority over the whole of the universe that He had created especially for His own purpose and plan.

I shall not perish personally, for I have absolutely no desire to join Satan and his fallen angels. As stated earlier, I have had far more than enough of him and his evil ways here on this earth. I certainly have no intention of staying in his company for eternity, for what a terrible situation that surely would be for anyone to have to try to endure, and yet there is no other alternative other than to endure it for this perishing is eternal!

I have certainly included myself in that wonderful "whosoever". I made certain of that fact as a teenager over fifty years ago when I made the life-changing decision to believe in Him. So now I not only believe in Him but I am also safe and very secure in Him as well.

As I write this very moment on my computer, there is a beautiful song also playing on the computer as well, confirming that very same reality for me. It is playing the words from that beautiful old hymn, "For I am sheltered safe within the arms of God". Therefore I shall never perish. God made certain of that fact for me when I accepted His offer of personal forgiveness from Himself for me personally, and I am determined to continue walking in that forgiveness on a daily basis. For that reason He therefore continues to guarantees my eternal future without any fear or doubt on my part whatsoever.

To protect any from perishing was and continues to be a major part of God's program and objective in the whole redemptive process. To provide that protection is very much a direct result of that love affair we have earlier talked about. Why would such a loving God ever want such a negative consequence to befall such objects of His eternal love, if He could in any way possible divert it from us? So He sends us to the world to point them towards the only sure answer, and to ensure they all know of that eternal redemption possibility.

CHAPTER 15

"But have everlasting life" The Eternal Results of His Love

✦

"For God so loved the world that He gave His only begotten Son that whosoever believeth in Him should not perish BUT HAVE EVERLASTING LIFE!" The songwriter beautifully wrote so many years ago; "When we've been there ten thousand years, bright shining as the sun; we have no less days to sing God's praise than the day we first begun". And another songwriter much later also wrote; "When you've been there a thousand years, a million maybe two, then look for me, for I will be there too!"

Once you are into eternity there will be no longer any hurry from there onward to go looking for me; for time as we now know it, will then be over forever, yet it will certainly still not be too late to come looking for me there, for we will then finally all be home in Father's house forever. I wonder as

"But have everlasting life" The Eternal Results of His Love

I write if that is not the ultimate example of "time standing still"!

What an exciting reality that will certainly be. I have caught a very slight glimpse of future glory from this side of my heavenly home, as I have even here now enjoyed my relationship with the King, but I surely am looking forward eagerly to going there to see Him some "day" face to face, and I sure hope you also have every intention of joining me there with Him as well. We are certainly all most welcome there for sure! God has surely made that fact so very clear for us.

I intentionally wrote the word "day" in that way in the previous paragraph, for what is a "day" in eternity where there is no night? And for that matter what are the "years" to which the song-writer referred to either when there are no "days"? "Everlasting" is all one eternal day! Think about that one, and for a while try to grasp it if really would like a real challenge, and you also want to have your mind totally overwhelmed as well.

Everlasting is forever, and when we have used up all of that forever, then there is another forever following immediately after that first one! You get the point for certain. If not, then I could just keep adding forevers here forever. In fact, my computer is telling me as I write here now that there is no such thing as a plural for "forever". I guess my computer thinks it is smarter that what I am. I also realize that you cannot even use the word "adding" when it comes to "forever". But I am going to ignore my computer's warning and write it that way anyway. So there; I have added "forevers" despite what my computer says!

Just try to imagine the reality of "everlasting life"! A lifetime of total bliss guaranteed and a "lifetime" there is forever. It is certainly hard to explain. And it is so wonderful when it is "everlasting LIFE" to which it refers. Do you love life here and now? Well if you do, then let me tell you something that is certainly so very exciting. If you have believed in Jesus, then despite the joys you experience here in doing so, you have still not experienced anything yet, in comparison to the "everlasting life" still awaiting you in your eternal future. Dream here for a while, and simply let your mind drift into "eternal bliss" and then try to imagine it. (OK! Come back now to today's realities!)

Remember this very crucial fact; the very best by far is yet to come for the actual believer, and it will then continue forever! That is certainly what Calvary has actually made possible for us as believers in Him, so revel in those future realities even as you still wait patiently here for their eternal fulfillment. Just the dreaming and the expectation is itself so very exciting, so do not stop dreaming, just dream on. You are certainly not going to exhaust the possibilities of "everlasting life" no matter how much you dream!

I am so very thankful for Calvary despite what we all did to Him there on that shameful day, for it was for all our sins that the Father allowed Him to be crucified, so we all stand equally guilty for that event that day.

I am also so glad that Jesus actually rebuked Peter on that day when he objected to Jesus' statement that He was going to Jerusalem to be rejected and then crucified there, and that despite Peter's objection, He still set His face with such determination in that direction, even though He fully realized in advance what was awaiting Him there on Mount Calvary in just a few days. Nothing could change His mind now. In fact, God never changes His mind anyway. It had been planned from before creation, so there certainly would be no backing down now on that eternal plan.

That amazing reality is also our driving force as we reach out to the world, and it is certainly our message to the world as well. That message is quite simply asking the world a very basic question. "Do you want to have eternal life, beyond anything you could ever dream? If you do, then all you need do is to actually believe in Jesus and it is yours for the asking, including all of the wonderful promises God has made for eternity for anyone who simply does so."

After that crucifixion of such an otherwise innocent Person; innocent of course except for our sins He was carrying on Him that day, they took His blood stained, lifeless body down from the cross before the dawning of Saturday, because they were afraid that His blood, falling upon the soil of the holy city of Jerusalem, would pollute the soil of that holy city on their Sabbath.

Yet if they had only known that day that His blood certainly does not pollute. In fact, it is the only fully guaranteed, permanent sin-stain remover available anywhere, and certainly also the only provision available to anyone for changing eternal perishing to eternal life for themselves. That is quite a "sales pitch" for Calvary for sure. And I suspect you will certainly agree on that one. There is nothing else available anywhere "on the market" that comes even close to comparing to it.

What a day that will be when each of us individually take our first step into eternity! Our finite, and so very limited minds, are actually totally incapable of coming close to grasping anything close to its actual reality, even in its most basic details, much less fathoming the full magnitude and scope of that future existence.

We can always dream and then dream some more. If fact, you can dream as much as you want, and you can still be assured that when you do eventually get home, the reality there will not fall short of your expectations. Actually, things there will far eclipse even our wildest dreams we have here of what heaven will be like that day.

Everlasting life has to do with far more that simply living forever. Everlasting means unending for certain, but in this context it is such a fully loaded word, and also involves so much more than simply a measuring of a period of time. In fact, everlasting life in relationship to our heavenly existence covers realities we cannot even imagine here.

It is certainly an all encompassing expression that includes benefits, blessings, and realities beyond imagining such as worshiping of the King face to face, together forever with the church of all the ages and also including a million other wonderful possibilities, and as yet totally unimaginable realities then awaiting us there in heaven that day as well.

Most of these other blessings we cannot even imagine in our present state. How can we possibly understand eternity's blessings and pleasures with only our earthly experience as a reference point to try to grasp these eternal realities awaiting us all there on that glorious day.

"But have everlasting life" The Eternal Results of His Love

It is far more difficult than trying to explain the beauty of a rose to someone who has been blind from birth. How do you explain color to someone who has never seen such awesome beauty as actual color? Just close your eyes and then try to imagine color with no reference for it even having entered your mind. It is no wonder we cannot come close to grasping the extent of that concluding phrase in this verse; "have everlasting life".

So we are yet totally blind here to heaven's awesome beauty, and to its amazing future realities. Someday however our eternal eyes will be fully opened for us and we will then be given "full vision" of heaven's glorious colors and beauty. What a glorious day that will surely be for us then when heaven's realities are fully there for us to see and to enjoy.

We often sing of gates of pearl, walls of jasper and also of streets of gold. I once somewhere heard it jokingly said that God first paved the streets of heaven with gold and then, when the job was finished, He swept up the gold dust and dumped it on earth and we have been fighting for it for many centuries since that day. There will be plenty of gold there for sure. It will be a massive city with its streets paved with it!

There are also gates of pearl there as well, but once I get inside the city I will not likely spend much of my time standing there at the gates. I have to admit I have always loved to travel, and that I have done it many, many times on a worldwide basis for the last 40 years of my previous world missions job before retirement, since that travel was a vital part of my actual job there, but I do not expect to be wanting to get out of the gates of this City once I am safely inside there. My travel days will be over!

Maybe I will actually take a quick visit now and then to the inside of the gates to welcome someone special to me into the city for their first time, but I will certainly not stay there for any extended period of time. There will certainly be other attractions inside that city far more important to me than the gates. Maybe that is because although I have travelled the world extensively for most of my life I am still a terrible tourist!

Two things I certainly do want to see in heaven as soon as I get there, and neither of these are made of gold, jasper, pearl or crystal, nor do they involve walls, gates, seas, streets or mansions!

Instead, firstly, I want to see Jesus and to spend a little while with Him. I said "a little while" because when you are talking eternity, a million years is only a "little while" anyway. So I certainly will spend "a little while" near Him. I sure hope you do not have to stand too long in line behind me to also do so!

Next I want to see and meet my worldwide family. I just cannot wait to see all of you there, and I am so looking forward to that "day" when I actually do see all of you there face to face. Actually I can hardly wait for that meeting of all of us in His holy presence.

I cry, "Come, Lord Jesus, come; for I am so very excited and really anxious to get home with my entire heavenly family." If I may do so, let me close this paragraph with a little slang we are all likely guilty of having used many times over ourselves; "See ya there!"

The song says, "Jesus, I belong to you..." but it is not simply the words of a beautiful song; in fact I do actually belong to Him for sure. These words

"But have everlasting life" The Eternal Results of His Love

are not just beautiful poetic language; it is also an amazing personal reality for me as well. First of all He made me so that fact rightfully gives Him ownership anyway. Then, because I was away from Him in terrible debt, he paid the price to repurchase me after I strayed from Him and got into serious trouble! That repurchasing is also for anyone who wants inclusion for themselves as well.

I am twice owned by Him; first created and then later lovingly redeemed by Him! What a privilege to "twice" belong to the King. That is real ownership for sure, and I am certainly not disputing His claim on me that I am actually twice owned by the King. In fact, I do not dispute even the Creator aspect of His ownership. Who would ever object anyway to being part of that ultimate Royal Family?

A little girl one day lost her beautiful little doll that she and her mom had together made for her and she was naturally broken hearted by that sad lost. But some days later, as she was walking in front of a second hand store, she there saw her lost doll actually for sale in the store window. So naturally she went inside, and there explained to the shopkeeper that it was actually her doll that she had made and had later lost, hoping they would give it back to her, because it was hers to begin with because she and her mom had made it.

But instead of receiving her precious doll back for free, they still insisted she had to pay the price they were demanding for it if she wanted the doll back. So she quickly ran home to mom, got some money and then immediately came hurrying back to the store, dropped the money she was clutching in her tiny hand down on the store counter and bought back for herself the precious doll she loved so much anyway but had then so sadly lost.

As she was leaving the store she was lovingly hugging her once lost, but now found and also repurchased doll, and was heard saying to the doll, "Now you are twice mine; I first made you so you were mine then, but now I have also bought you as well!" There is certainly no need for me to here explain that illustration for anyone!

We also are "twice His". He made us and then He bought us. And these are two very exciting realities for us; His times two! We are His first of all by creation, but then also His by redemption as well. This is such a wonderful reality for us as we serve Him here, and then also as we look towards eternity with the confidence such a relationship so easily inspires in us.

I am not merely an "heir", waiting for Him to pass off the scene so that I will then be able to inherit, for He is eternal! I am in full ownership of all that is His right from the moment I became part of His family. It is all mine already, but it is also all yours as well if you have also believed on Him, and that certainly does not in any way diminish my supply whatsoever. It all belongs to all of us all of the time, and there is certainly more than enough for everyone. This is not about having to share a limited supply. Instead it is actually about all of us tapping into an unlimited supply for ourselves, and then sharing it with others as well.

He is my Father, my Director, my Administrator, my Financial Manager, my Daily Planner, my Security Guard and everything else that I could ever need Him to be here and now, for I am totally His. So I just simply follow Him. He knows the end from the beginning so what better Administrator could I ever want or need in my life for today? There are no surprises for Him. He knows all the actual ends from all of the actual beginnings of everything relating to me.

If you have not already done so as yet, then simply say to Him, "Lord, I am now ready to respond to You even in the here and now, because I so want my "everlasting life" to begin here immediately". And once you do so, it will begin at that very point. It has been a reality for me personally since the night I first believed in Him, and there is still no end to it in sight as yet. In fact, there will never be any termination of that personal relationship between both of us, because that is just the way we certainly both want it to be, and also to remain so through both time as well as eternity.

He is my Shepherd and I am just so delighted to be one of His precious prized sheep, and that certainly suits me just fine. A pastor once asked a group of young kids if any of them would like to quote Psalm 23 for the congregation, and a very young girl raised her hand and started to wave it excitedly so she could get his attention. She actually surprised him because she was so young, so he asked her to come to the platform and quote it for them. She bravely came up front, put her tiny hands behind her back, smiled broadly at the pastor and he smiled back at her and she quoted: "The Lord is my Shepherd and there is nothing else I want!" Then she smiled again and sat down; she was finished!

Actually she was right on. What other relationship is there that will guarantee for us that it will be all we will ever need for both time and also for eternity? He is everything here, and will certainly be everything there as well, and there surely is nothing else I need or even want for here today or for eternity either.

I am so extremely happy to take my chances on His interpretation of what everlasting life will include for me over there when I see Him face to face. I certainly do not expect any disappointments on my part on that one for sure. In fact, it will be far beyond my expectations even when I dream of heaven.

He is my Shepherd while I am still out in the field, and totally exposed to the dangerous realities of that field; the wolves, lions, storms and many other such things, but He is also my Shepherd who is leading me into the safety of that eternal "sheepfold" where I will experience all that is included in the expression in that promise of this verse of being assured of "everlasting life".

No wonder we live with our eyes focused upon the heavens for the opening of that gate for each of us individually (death) or for all of us collectively (rapture) could take place at any time, for as the song so correctly states, "This could be the dawning of that grand and glorious day." And that would be so very wonderful if this were actually that very day! "Come, Lord, come, and do so as soon as possible" (AKA ASAP) I have had all I want from Satan forever, and I am now eagerly watching for Jesus now to come and get me!

So "everlasting life" starts with abundant life here, and then continues into eternity with realities that are far beyond anything we could ever expect, or even dream in the wildest stretches of our imaginations. Does this present reality, as well as these yet future expectations interest you in any way? If they do, then be sure that you are guaranteed inclusion by simply meeting the stated qualifications for inclusion; simply believe in Him. He is patiently, but also anxiously waiting right now for a "yes" response from anyone! If you do so, then I will surely see you there!

SECTION TWO

JOHN 3:16 AND WORLD MISSIONS

INTRODUCTION

God's love for the world that took Him to the extremes of Calvary that day, as well as the primary mission and challenge of the church since that very day, are so intertwined with each other they are inseparable. If there were no Calvary, then certainly there would also be no message of hope for the world. Also from the other direction, if there was no world missions challenge from God for us to go; then there would be no messengers to the world to share that story of Calvary's great love for them.

These two are therefore both fully interconnected and motivated by these two realities; God loves the whole world, and He is surely the only solution to the world's eternal needs as well. These are the most basic motivations relating to God's salvation message for this lost world, and they certainly also are the most basic realities and motivations which inspire the church's passionate commitment to world missions as well.

On that basis therefore, missions is certainly no more of an "extracurricular activity" for the church, than what Calvary actually was just "something extra He needed to do" for God to reach out to us. They both are priority one for both God, and for the entire church as well through the centuries.

We should therefore never even think of demoting either one of them to a secondary position or role. The two are together the number one objectives even today for both God, and also for us as His church as well.

We surely do need to keep the two of these in the forefront at all times. Calvary certainly is the very central core of our message to the world, for it is the only source of help for any of us, and that is the great message we have to share with the world! Coupled with that in total unity is the fact the fact that the provision and message without the messenger is unable to accomplish God's ultimate intentions, but together they will mean freedom, forgiveness and eternal life for millions

We therefore need to be in full agreement with Him as members of His church on this challenge. That is why we often refer to this challenge as "the great commission", because it was certainly given to us by Him from that very crucial perspective, and also carried that weight of needing to be taken seriously by the whole church, and consequently followed to the very "letter of the word" in fulfilling its worldwide mandate.

This is not just another alternative for getting a message of hope out to the world. Instead, this is the only option for getting this only life-changing message out there, and sharing with the world the total redemption costs to God, and also the complete covering provided through Calvary for the world. He gave and died; therefore we give and go.

Calvary is everything for the church, for Calvary certainly does cover it all for us, but Calvary is also certainly everything for the whole world as well. I am sure that fact hardly needs to be stated here to

INTRODUCTION

any Christian. There is only one "cure" and only one solution and redemption offered for everyone, and that reality is our total challenge, motivation, passion and also our message to the world. Therefore, it is for this very obvious reason that I have added this extra review of John 3:16 here as it relates to the church's mission to the world. For that is certainly what this whole verse is all about.

John 3:16, despite all of its wonderful revelations and realities, is totally non-effective without world missions to make its message known, and thereby making its love relevant to the needs of today's society. The Gospel is personal, and choosing to respond to its message is also personal. So the world must know these realities, and then make their own individual decisions regarding the gospel's offer of total pardons for all who will then ask personally for inclusion, and also for its miraculous covering.

So the challenge is quite simple. If you have the message, then you must run as fast and as far as possible with it into the world, for this great offer has a very serious "expiry date" attached to it! Therefore the offer will some day be withdrawn, and from then onwards it will tragically be forever too late for anyone still outside its protection to take advantage of its provision.

That is the challenge of world missions we are faced with today. It is either now or never for our world, therefore we all really need to get very serious about making it "now" for certain, because the alternative "never" certainly presents an extremely desolate eternal future for anyone.

So our challenge today is to take this message of His love, and the sacrifice He so willing made, as well as His offer of eternal redemption into our total world. That total world is certainly across the seas to the nations of our world, but on a more personal daily basis, it is also across our streets, across our workplaces, across our classrooms and even across our very own tables. Wherever there is a needy soul there is certainly a personal, private "mission field" for us to reach out to with His love.

That is the challenge the church has been commissioned by God Himself to be taken seriously on a personal basic by each of His followers.

Number One   "For God"

THE SOURCE OF WORLD MISSIONS

The original source, and certainly also the greatest promoter and motivator behind the challenge of world missions to our whole world, which is also undoubtedly so much a part of the commission of the universal church today, is actually none other than God Himself. This is where it all started; with God in the actual throne room of heaven.

The Triune God, in total and complete agreement, made the world changing decision that the Son would become the first "missionary" to our needy world, when it was there felt by God Himself that He had no other choice other than to get personally involved with, and also for us, in our very desperate and otherwise hopeless situation.

Consequently, God made the decision to come from the security of where He was, to the danger, filth and vile corruption of where we were to help us. That is where the missions outreach to our world actually started, when God made that first move in love towards us.

So world missions undeniably started with Him. He surely became the originator of the whole process, and we now gladly join Him as a church in continuing to actually expand that outreach of His love to our world today. "Do as I do, not simply. do as I say" is God's mission comment to His total church today.

As a result, the church today has no other choice but to pick up that torch He lit twenty centuries ago at Calvary, and now run with it as fast and as far as possible into our entire needy world. It certainly did start with God, but we are all very much aware of the reality that He then passed the commission on to His church, and since it is the sovereign God whom we serve, we must answer His call and commission gladly to go to make disciples for Him no matter what the personal cost may be to ourselves.

We have certainly been drafted by Him, and are now very much part of His army. So His orders to us are quite basic; into the whole world for every one of His followers is the call, whether that world is across the seas or across the street. And there will be no future call from Him for any retreat either. The only other call we will hear, will be the call from Him at the end of the age for us all to "come on home now. The task is over for you forever. So come and enjoy eternity with me, for I am anxiously waiting for you to join Me here!"

He paid no attention to personal costs to Himself in His coming to our world, so He quite naturally has the same expectations from us as well. At any cost to everyone, whether that is across the street or across the world. As the worship songs states, "There are no unknown soldiers in the army of the Lord!" We are all personally known by Him, and

He keeps great records of our involvement in this great battlefield. Rewards are therefore awaiting us in heaven for our services to Him on the battleground here.

So the world missions assignment was not a "later addition" to the church's marching orders from God. Instead it was very much a vital part of the very core of God's original plan from all eternity. After all, of what value is a cure for any serious problem, if the afflicted ones never hear of that cure being readily available for them? Even a "miracle drug" left unused on the pharmacy shelf accomplishes absolutely nothing for the afflicted. And for certain, Calvary's atonement can surely be considered a "miracle drug" for today's society.

God started the outreach to the world, motivated by His love for that world, and then commissioned, or should it actually be ordered, us to join Him in pushing as far as possible into Satan's "confiscated" territory with that message of His love, and also the solution He had so costly provided to get us away from Satan's control, and then from there safely into God's own loving arms.

It actually should not be too difficult for the church to enthusiastically embrace that challenge from God, and go with a passion to the world with that exciting message. When we are actually excited about something, it is not too difficult to get anyone to talk about it. So as the song says, we must, "get all excited, go tell everybody that Jesus Christ is still the King of Kings".

In Mark 16:15 Jesus says, "Go ye into all the world, and preach the gospel to every creature". (Also Matthew 28:18-20 states a similar challenge from Jesus as well) His listeners that day certainly had no idea how big that world actually was, because so little of it had been discovered at that time, but Jesus Himself certainly did know its size and numbers, and was thinking of it all when He gave the church His commission that day.

We sing, "When He was on the cross I was on His mind, and that certainly is comforting for us. But it was not exclusively us on His mind that day. The whole world was the central focus of His thinking there, for it was not a limited atonement He made there that day. His love was just that all encompassing, and so also was His thinking as well in relationship to that sacrifice He was making for the sins of the whole world.

So the message of missions is not about condemnation here or about any future judgment either, although we certainly know these realities do exist. Instead it is about God's love and forgiveness here, and also His offer of abundant life for eternity, instead of any of the alternative negative possibilities. And who would not want to be a bearer of such great news? So our response to His commission is not a "chore" for the church. It is instead a delight for every believer to get into the action and go.

The world desperately needs to hear that message, and God has clearly given His instructions, and also His full and complete authority to us to be sure they do hear of it from us. We do have His personal commission and full authority to go anywhere and everywhere with its message, and for certain nobody therefore has any right to tell us we cannot reach into their nation, tribe or family with that message, because the King has told us to do so, and certainly nobody has any authority to try to override the King's commands on anything at any time. We have His full authorization and authority to go, so that is just what we intend to do. It is into the whole world no matter what the barriers may be!

That is missions in its simplest, most basic form; sharing with the world the real picture of God as loving us all. Therefore we are now doing just that at His request, and in fact, doing so as already stated at His actual command! It all started with Him, and we are just so delighted to actually be personally included in His love. Then to have been given the wonderful personal privilege to be actually expressing and sharing that love out there to the whole world is fantastic, for that is a challenge and also a joy for us beyond measure.

He is now waiting for our "salute" and our "Yes, Sir!" to His orders. Then just listen to Him telling us to "march"!

Number Two   "So Loved"

THE MOTIVATION OF WORLD MISSIONS

What a motivation love challenges us with here anyway, for us to go to our own sin-sick world with it, and also because of it as well! But when it is actually about God's love, and it also includes the amazing fact that God loves them despite anything and everything that has messed with their lives, it surely does become a motivation beyond any possible comparison whatsoever for us.

He came because of His love, and we now go to our world that He "so loved" because of that same love. It is our message, and also our motivation as well to go out to the world that He actually does "so love". The fact that He so loves the world surely does "take my breath away", but that fact also drives me into that same world with its liberating message as well.

Fear is certainly a strong motivation in itself, and seeing danger is an easily understood reason for anyone to run. But there is no greater driving force than love. Fear may make you run for shelter and safety for yourself, but love will make you run so very much faster as well as further towards, and also for, someone who is the actual object of that love.

To hear someone yell "fire" in a building where you are standing would make anyone run, but still there is no motivation that is any stronger than that of love. Imagine pulling into the driveway of your house, and as you are getting out of the car, you suddenly see smoke pouring out of the windows of your home, and you realize in a panic that your young child in still inside that now burning house. What would you do?

I strongly suspect that what you just saw coming out through the house windows would really make you run rapidly to the burning house, and probably not even take the time to close your car door! Your love for your child in such danger throws personal fears regarding self totally aside, as that love you have for your child suddenly takes over completely.

So we quite naturally run with love, to love, for love and also because of love. Therefore it is God's love for our needy world that is the greatest and most powerful motivation behind our world mission commission and passion; because He loves them, and also because we love Him. So we therefore most naturally love them as well, and run passionately to also help them. That is actually the Great Commission from God to the church in its most basic setting; take the message of His love and run into the world with it until all have had a chance to hear.

The God that we love, and so willingly serve, and who has brought us so many personal benefits and blessings for both here and certainly for eternity, "needs" for us to let the world know that He so loves them also. And so we pick up that great challenge to do as He surely did, and that is to go with His love to the world to help them there in their need.

The word need in reference to God may sound quite strange, for how can God need anything, yet in relationship to world missions it is most certainly a reality. He needs our commitment, and He needs our involvement as well, and these are two extremely challenging realities for us. Yet at the same time as His needing our commitment to share with them His protective love, He also desperately needs their loving response to His love in return as well.

So our challenge is not simply to go tell them. It also includes bringing them to God and to His love, so they come to know His love for themselves personally, and can then return their love to Him for that very reason that He does love them so very much Himself.

So world missions is about meeting the world's need for His love for certain, but it is also in a very real way about meeting God's need for their love in return as well. As I just mentioned, God and personal need do not seem to belong together, until you then add the word love to that combination. God has a great need to have the objects of His love back in His family! There is God and need together in just one statement, and certainly a statement easy enough to believe for sure. It is, and always has been, the total priority and motivation behind His actions throughout the ages.

Therefore the message we are commanded to take to the world is an extremely exciting one for certain. This is surely not a message we dread or fear to have to share with them. In actual fact, it is to the extreme in the very opposite direction.

There is nothing to be feared or avoided in telling someone they are loved!

Try this one: "So, my friend, did you know that God loves you passionately and desperately wants you to know it and He wants you to then respond to Him? If you did not already know, or if you have neglected to consider it, then let me tell you that it is true for He really loves you."

That wonderful reality is a tremendous motivation for us to go into the world with this message from three different and very distinct perspectives. The first reality is that God actually does love them for sure, and He certainly wants them all to know that fact. He loves them, so we shout it out with all the excitement and enthusiasm such a message deserves. There is no uncertainty or caution here on this one whatsoever.

This is it. God loves them and there is nothing more important to God than the challenge that everyone knows that thrilling reality. So we go with this very simple, and yet so profound message; "God sent me to you and told me to tell you that He loves you!" That is our message to the whole world as we respond to His love to them and also to His commission to us as well.

Secondly, the world needs to know because their need is so desperate whether they even realize it themselves or not, and that love God has for them is the only answer to their need or solution to their problem. And what a wonderful, exciting solution it actually is to be able to tell the world that the only one who can "fix" their problem is actually reaching out to them in love to do just that for them with "no questions asked".

God is basically saying to them, "I do not need for you to tell me about your sins or your past life, I just want to talk to you about a new beginning. It will be like being born all over again for you!" And that is our message; the possibility for anyone to be "born again" and start all over anew.

Then thirdly, because we ourselves as followers of Jesus need to obey God's commission and calling, and thereby show Him our commitment and allegiance to Him by obeying His "marching orders" into the world, and by doing so giving ourselves to extending the reach of His love as widely as possible.

How can we possibly disobey our Master and Lord? Nobody, who is a true follower of the King, can answer Him with a; "not now – maybe later" answer! No further postponing of the sharing of this love affair possible for any genuine follower of His. It has to be a "yes, Sir" immediate response to Him instead from us.

His love is our motive as well as being our message to the world. It is a time for our rejoicing and shouting the joy of that love out there, whether it is across the office, factory, classroom or seas! Grab a trumpet and shout it out to the whole world. "GOD LOVES YOU!"

That really is so much better that having to go to the world to just warn them of God's coming judgment. So, despite the reality of that future judgment, the motivation for us is that God does not want for it to fall on anyone, simply because He loves them, and therefore has provided a way of escape, but not just an escape from a very sad reality, but also an escape into another most wonderful one! That

is our motivation for going; that God really does "so love" them.

Number Three   *"The World"*

THE OBJECTIVE OF WORLD MISSIONS

The Gospel message of God's love is not only for a selected, chosen few in our world, and it is certainly not confined solely to us by any means. It is instead a message to be shouted to the whole wide world. There are none exempted no matter who they are or where they may presently live; from the world's most massive cities even to its most remote and isolated tiny, hidden, distant villages. It is for the whole world because God's love is so abundant it overflows to all of them no matter who they are, or where they may actually live. It is simply worldwide, and that is certainly all inclusive in my thinking.

"The world" is not a selective term. Therefore the church certainly has no right to be selective in any way whatsoever in its outreach either. It is all inclusive, and reaches in both directions; back to eternity past and forward to eternity future and includes every created being in that whole time span. The whole world was the total target of His love, and also the reason for His dying on Calvary, therefore it must likewise be the scope of our outreach focus as well.

It is quite a challenge we have been given, to ensure all who are part of our present world now have a chance to hear of His love, and to then respond to it for forgiveness and inclusion in its scope and influence. There is nothing we can do for past generations. They are beyond our reach, but this generation is still totally our responsibility, and well within our present reach. Someday we will answer to God as to what we did to share His love with them. I am personally certain that I want to be ready myself to answer Him on that one that day.

Since His love for the world is universal, therefore the church certainly needs to go with the message to exactly the same extreme. Every race, every nationality, every language; all are included and none are ever excluded for certain. "The world" is the whole world and there is no reason for any question on that fact! God certainly has no favorites, so when He tells us He loves the world, then there is certainly no need to waste time by asking God for clarification as to whom He includes in that word. The world is simply the world.

So our challenge is to reach our neighbor, our town, our nation and also the whole world with the same passion shown for all of them. There are no "blank spots" in this love affair by God, and also no exception in His commission to us either! It is every one of His followers to the whole world!

No "coping out" is ever permitted on the part of any follower of Jesus. We all have to find a way to be involved in that worldwide task and there are no minor roles in the job. Whether it is going around the world or praying as you sit in a wheelchair unable to move, your role in the harvest is still a major one!

"The world" that He "so loved" and continues to "so love" certainly includes every religions group in the world, and it is as strong for them as it if for the most devout Christians in our world today as well. But can you just imagine how His heart must ache for them to some day hear of and then passionately respond to His love He has for them?

Even the atheists of any society are also included, despite their denying the existence of any supernatural being whatsoever. Simply denying the fact of His existence does not negate His love for them. They are all included in the same love affair of our Savior, so the objective of world missions is obviously that we go to them that they also will all be reached, and lovingly presented with His provision and personal invitation to come back home to Him.

"The world" is quite a massive task, and certainly presents us with an enormous challenge for today, but the church must definitely not be deterred, discouraged, distracted or overwhelmed by its enormity. God certainly loved it all in its entirety. So the message of His love is certainly for all, and His promise to also go with us as we go to the world is for all of the church as well. That also includes His promise to us to give all of us the "Spirit-anointed" ability to do so for Him with capacities far beyond our own abilities.

We must go to the whole world with His love story no matter what the personal cost may be to ourselves. I heard a story somewhere recently of a young, new recruit into the coastguard who was on his first actual assignment into a fierce storm at sea to rescue the occupants of a ship in serious distress. The young sailor was very nervous and quite scared as they moved out into that storm to assist the vessel. He turned to the captain of the coastguard boat and said, "If we go out there in that storm to help, we will never get back home to safety again." The captain's reply to him was simply, "Young man, as coastguard sailors we do not have to get back safely ourselves but we certainly do have to go out!"

And so it is for the church. No matter what the potential personal cost may be to us as we head out into the storm, we do have to "go out". Since the world is the object of His love, then naturally the world is also the object of our mission as well. So certainly the association here of these two factors with our challenge as a church, is really not all that difficult for the church to grasp and accept.

Number Four   *"That He Gave"*

THE ACTION OF WORLD MISSIONS

✨

World missions is undeniably about giving for certain, but before anyone assumes I am here referring to money, just wait for a minute. It all started with God giving His only Son to rescue our lost world, and that is surely the ultimate in giving for certain. In fact, no act of giving throughout the whole of history has come close to that Gift in cost to its donor, nor in total value to those who have received that Gift for themselves.

Giving in relationship to God is certainly not a one-time event, but this one act of giving on His part certainly was, and I am so very glad that it was only needed to be given just this one time, for the whole of the human race from creation until this present day.

But this time when God gave He really excelled, and went so far beyond any gift before or since in the expression of His love for us. He set quite a standard for us all for real genuine giving, when He gave us this Gift. His Son was the very center of His heart, yet He was freely given to prove God's point that He really did "so love the world" as well!

So the very first act of giving to "world missions" was a Gift from God Himself, and in so doing He set the standard pretty high for us as well. His gift certainly was not mere surplus from heaven. It was instead the very essence of who He is Himself, and that is the extremely high standard God now sets for our giving to Him, and to the world as well!

That giving also extended into my own life personally as well. As I knelt at an altar in my home church to give my heart to the Lord one Thursday night, while I was still a teenager, one of my former high school classmates came and knelt there beside me to pray with me.

He then opened his Bible and spread it out on the altar before me as I knelt there with my eyes filled with tears. He put his finger on only one verse on the page before me and said to me, "Read this verse because this is what God told me that He wants for you to know tonight." He was actually pointing at II Cor. 4:3, and it read in his KJV Bible "But if our gospel be hid it is hid to them that are lost." That reality got me then and there for certain, and I have never since been able to get away from its challenge to me.

From that very first night I felt the call of God on my personal life for world missions, so I also gave myself to the challenge it presented. I gave my life to God that night for certain, but also to His mission for the world, to share Him and His great love where possible.

After college and marriage I acted upon that commitment to Him for the world, but at that time it was primarily for southern Africa (Zambia first then also South Africa & later Malawi), and I certainly have never regretted that exciting decision I made. In fact, had I known then what I now know of what God was preparing to do in Zambia, I would have been "uncontrollably" excited about heading there at that time, instead of being somewhat nervous as I was that night flying south over Africa for my very first time in August of 1972.

I well remember that first night flying south over the Sahara Dessert of North Africa, and looking out of the plane window all night because I could not sleep. All I could see was an occasional camp fire burning in the darken dessert. I still remember thinking that night; "what am I getting myself involved in here?" I admit I was nervous about the uncertainty for me and my wife that lay south of us that night as we flew.

We arrived in Zambia on August 6, 1972. The national church we worked with there had about twenty-five tiny congregations in the whole nation at that time. But today, at the time of my writing this some forty years later, that national church is running close to two thousand congregations, many of them very large, and now having to have two or three Sunday services in a row just to handle their congregations. "Thank You, God, so very much for allowing me to play a small part in causing that to happen in that nation!"

God found a way for me to give, and so I gave my life to missions. But we all stand equally responsible for our world, and must also each find a way to give God's love to them as well. Sharing His amazing love with the world is such an exciting task, and for the giver it turns into an extremely exciting life as well. This is not simply a one-sided benefit to a lost world which of course it is for sure, but it is also the source of the giver's greatest joy as well.

So giving should become a most natural reflex for us all; both giving to God and also giving to our world as well, especially when we surely realize that we ourselves are so obviously blessed with the very best of both worlds. We certainly cannot deny the very obvious fact that we do have the very best of this present world in our society where we live, but at the same time, and this is even more exciting for us, we also have the very best of the world to come; that being the hope of eternal life, which is a blessing far beyond anything we can presently have or even try to grasp or imagine.

We ourselves are surely blessed times two if that sentence makes any sense to you. But whether it does or not, the idea is certainly correct! The song says, "I have everything I need to make me happy. I have Jesus to show me the way." And that is so true. We have everything in Him, but we also have everything else here in this life as well. How much more can we possibly be blessed, than to personally have these two realities combined for us as we certainly do now have?

Yet so much of our present world has neither; absolutely nothing here, and dying of hunger daily as a result, but even more tragically, having nothing ahead for them either for eternity except to actually "perish", because they have not heard of the alternative He has provided.

What a tragedy, and that is an understatement for sure to simply call it a tragedy. It is such a million times over, for it is eternal. "Oh, God, how will we ever answer You if we do not also give; give our lives, give our resources, give our time, give our prayers and also give our compassion to this world You tell us so very clearly that You certainly do so love"?

He gave so we must also follow His example as well. But that giving on our part should not be looked upon as an exception, or even considered by ourselves or by anyone else as a rare commitment by us in any way. It should instead be the natural life-style of every follower of Jesus who is in any way convinced that He is indeed the only hope for our world, and the only way to eternal life for them as well. How can we possibly keep the only answer to ourselves? "Only" is extremely exclusive. So the only answer must become available worldwide!

Jonas Salk discovered the vaccine for polio in the early 1950's at the height of the polio epidemic raging at that time and I still remember those polio scares from my young years as a kid. But what would have happened if he had simply kept that vaccine to himself, instead of sharing that great cure with the world? That terrible disease had caused so many deaths everywhere, so the world was in dire need of it.

But just suppose he had kept it a total secret to himself, and did not let it be known to the world so very much in need of it? It would have been totally useless, unless it was shared. I may actually have contacted it and died from it myself had the vaccine not been made available at that time! It was just that serious. But it was certainly eagerly shared with the world, and also fully utilized in that day, and polio was finally actually beaten by that sharing!

How can we not give, and what excuse would we ever be able to use to answer God when He asked us that day when we all stand eternally in His presence?

The Action of World Missions

"I gave to and for the world, but why did you not feel any great need to also give as well?" I surely never want to have to answer that question myself.

God gave and certainly any act of giving on God's part is exciting, but this act of giving, combined with the Gift itself, and the extreme extent to which it was also actually given, has certainly become the central attraction of history since the day it was first given on a mount just outside the walls of the city of Jerusalem over two thousand years ago.

God's reaction to His great love for the world was certainly to give, and so any giving of any kind associated with world missions should not in any way be considered simply as an obligation or expectation. It also should be done totally as an act of personal love on our part for God, and also for the very world He so passionately loves. What more can we do when He gave so much to us and to our world? Giving is a reflex action to love as it certainly was for God, but it also should be just as natural a reflex action to us, as well as a natural response of our love for Him and for our world also.

Number Five   *"His Only Begotten Son"*

THE SUPREME SOLUTION OF WORLD MISSIONS

When the "offering plate" was passed to God on "missions Sunday", He willingly placed His only begotten Son inside, and never went later to get any change back, or ask for any kind of a refund whatsoever. This was His very best Gift He could ever give to show His love for the world despite God's unlimited giving potential He certainly possesses as the Creator of everything.

Also in that process of His showing that love in the giving of that Gift, He actually provided the only salvation solution ever to have been made available to us, with the capacity to change any person's eternal destiny from perishing to eternal life. So that was certainly quite a long-term Gift He gave that day.

God's gift to the world, and to His mission to reach out in love to it, was certainly far more than a few dollars occasionally dropped in the church offering plate designated as missions, and that kind of giving is certainly also very important as well in the process of reaching out to our world. I am certainly not denying that important fact. Actually, such continued serious giving is an absolute imperative if we are going to keep that reaching out to our world in the forefront as the loving church of Jesus Christ.

But this Gift that God gave to reach our world, was in fact, the very essence of who God is in Person, and that Gift cost Him oh so dearly to give, but it also should be noted that the cost did not catch God by surprise by any means. There are certainly no surprises with God on anything. He knew that high cost in full right from the very beginning.

But even though He knew that actual cost in full before He even made the decision, or began the process to execute the plan He had already made to give that Gift, He had certainly fully checked out the "price tag" on the Gift well ahead of the time. Yet He still did not falter even for a moment in His giving of that Gift of His only begotten Son despite the extreme cost to Him and to His Son as well in the giving of that Gift.

The Gift was far, far more than simply one gift out of His abundance. The Gift was an "only one available" type of Gift; the only one of its kind anywhere, with none other coming even close to it to be found anywhere in the entire universe. So it was certainly an extremely unique Gift that He gave to the world that day, for it was a Gift out of His own very essence; a part of His very self. It was certainly a Gift from His heart for it was His very heart in essence that He gave. That is both a Gift and also an act of giving like none other.

God was actually giving Himself as a Gift to the world to express His love for the world. That is certainly giving to the greatest possible limits of any concept of giving. I surely do not expect there will be any objections whatsoever to that last statement. God certainly pushed giving to the very limit when He gave that Gift, and we still look back with great respect, and also in total awe even over two thousands years of past history at that amazing act of His giving there on Calvary that day.

We really have no idea ourselves whatsoever as to what that Gift actually did cost God for Him to give it to us. We may even try to fathom giving a gift like God's giving of His only Son, and actually even acknowledge that such a gift would really cost us as well, if we gave our only son to such a death, because we also love them so much as well.

But we must remember that our capacity to love a son or a daughter is practically nothing when compared to God's capacity to love His only Son, and the actual giving costs involved that day for God were most certainly totally in line proportionally with the increased love God was capable of, and surely did have for His Son.

So today we also give ourselves, our lives, possessions and resources to Him and to our world, in full appreciation of His Gift to us and to our world, and even that is still so small and insignificant in comparison to and with this Gift which He gave to us. Our giving certainly needs to also follow His example, and therefore we should hold nothing back either. All we have is totally His anyway; our lives, our possessions, our time and everything we have, are, or could ever hope to be in the future.

Our world missions involvement is therefore primarily an expression of our love for Him, because He loves us, and because He also does love our world so much, we want them also to know of His love, both for their own benefit, but also so they can then return their love which He so yearns to have directly back to Him. Therefore world missions is simply encouraging the object of His love to accept it, and then to return that love to Him in full as well.

Number Six   *"That Whosoever"*

THE TOTAL RANGE OF WORLD MISSIONS

What a challenge there is contained in that word "whosoever". That means that every contact we have in every situation on every day of our lives are potential believers if we share with them and they choose to accept. The word leaves a personal choice as far as the accepting is concerned, and we certainly have little to say on that aspect of the word, but it also carries with it a tremendous personal challenge for the Christian.

God is not going to confront anyone. That is our assigned task as the church. Go to the world so that the "whosoever" who wishes to do so can actually respond to Him, and then enjoy all the benefits that He has provided for us through the cross.

While we have no say in who may comprise the "whosoever" who do respond, we ourselves do have to make the choices on the "whosoever" we choose to give the message to, and thereby offer them the opportunity to accept the pardon. This word certainly places a tremendous amount of responsibility of choice regarding who is going

The Total Range of World Missions

to be a responder to the "whosoever" right in our own hands. We make the choice as to who hears by making the choice as to whom we share the message with personally. And that is quite a responsibility entrusted to us.

There is no saying to God that we did not find anyone to give the message of His love to, for it is for whosoever will. So I am so glad we do not have to wonder about anyone as to whether they are included or not. If they want to accept His pardon, then it is theirs for the asking. It is just as simple as that to anybody. But we are obligated to give them the chance to make that personal choice for themselves, and that is the challenge we face as a church today, to give everyone an opportunity to be one of the "whosoever" who do choose to respond.

Therefore the message of world missions is to the "whosoever" in its scope and outreach. Anybody and everybody who wishes to respond are included in its invitation. The only limiting factor in its universal coverage is the personal choice of each individual for themselves, and that is certainly not a decision that we make the choice on for any other's personal inclusion.

We personally do not make any exceptions in the sharing. We need to reach everyone, from the terrorist to the orphan, and it is only then that their inclusion in the benefits of redemption becomes a personal choice for them. Since it is not something that we make the decision on ourselves, therefore it is not a factor we personally consider in deciding the direction of the exposure of the world to the message. It is whosoever, and they then have to personally choose inclusion in its invitation for themselves.

The message of missions and the exposure to that message is for everyone, but the actual benefits are only for whosoever who then chooses to reach out and personally accept the offer for themselves. That we cannot control, for it is certainly not our decision, but nevertheless we are responsible to give them a chance to make that personal decision for themselves at any time. That is something that we certainly can and do control. We do "control" its scope of availability, by controlling its actual distribution. Therefore we desperately need to "go" with the message.

Forgiveness is available for anybody and also for everybody, but is only effective in ensuring eternal changes in those who hear and then accept the offer. That is the challenge we face today as the church of Jesus Christ in participating in the thrilling task of reaching our world with the Gospel. It is certainly for everyone who will accept it with no exceptions whatsoever. If you want in on the offer, then it is all yours.

Number Seven   *"Believeth in Him"*

THE LIBERATING PROCLAMATION OF WORLD MISSIONS

Our message to the world through missions is quite simple and basic. Simply believe in Him. It is far too simple for anyone to say. "I am not really capable of doing such a thing." Ask even a tiny child if they want to believe in Him and they will often nod their head, smile and simply say, "Yes". The process is just that simple. No dramatic action is required to actually "believe". Just "nod your head" to Him and He will certainly get the message. That is all believing in Him actually takes to get anyone in.

    That is about the extent of the "believing in him" that the thief on the cross did as well, and it sure worked for him that day, although I doubt he actually even "nodded his head", for it would have been practically impossible for him to have done so on that cross, but his accepting Jesus was basically just that simple, and I am certain it is still working for him two thousand years later. He is still in paradise as a result of simply turning his attention for a moment to One who was also dying right there beside him that day. But that short, simply conversation that day changed his destiny for eternity. That is what simple believing in Him can do for anyone who actually does so.

He did not say much that day as he hung there dying on one of the outside crosses; he simply believed in the One dying there next to him on that center cross. But fortunately, for that thief that day, it was this very same "Him" of whom this verse actually speaks who was also hanging there beside him that day, and he was able to there reach out to Him for a future amazing hope for himself despite his desperate situation at that crucial time. He there became Calvary's very first convert after that act was accomplished.

Tell the world that once they believe in Him the offences are totally removed in the same manner as happened to that thief that day, and anyone who does so then stands before God justified – just as though they had never ever sinned. That is quite a radical transformation for one simple act of believing, but it certainly worked for the dying thief that day.

It also really worked for me as well so many years later as I also believed in Him, and He changed everything for me. I am so happy to now be able to tell the world that it will also work just as effectively for them as well as it did for me, and for that thief on that cross that day.

May I add here that I highly recommend it personally as a cure for the ills of this life today, and also as a protection from "perishing" for all of eternity for anyone who is interested in accepting that cure, and then having it applied to their own personal need as well? That is quite a wonderful message to freely offer to anyone who simply wants to accept it for themselves, and in so doing fully get in on the offer and the solution. There is nothing very complicated or difficult here for sure for anyone to grasp and fully understand.

There are actually some people who claim they simply cannot believe in someone or something they cannot see themselves. Such a person must have a very difficult time even breathing if they do not believe in invisible things, for oxygen is quite hard to actually see for yourself. They cannot believe in creation or in an actual Creator, yet everything around them is crying out, "I am another product of that Intelligent Designer."

I recently saw a cartoon of two snowmen talking and one is "saying" to the other one, "Don't be absurd. Nobody made us. We evolved by chance from snowflakes." Now that would certainly require some "believing" to believe. It is certainly so much easier to simply believe that a couple of kids rolled up the wet snow and stuck the carrots in the top for noses even if nobody saw them actually do it. So believing in Him is so much simpler for anyone than trying to prove there is no one "out there" and that there is no God.

So our message to the world is so much simpler to accept; just believe in Him. There is nothing too difficult or complicated about that simple, basic action of believing. Telling the world to "believe" is certainly not in any way a new message by any means. We practice believing many times over every day of our lives. Actually we even "believe" in our watches that they are telling us the truth and they usually do exactly that.

Believing in and trusting are both very much a part of our everyday living. We drive fearlessly through a green light because we believe that the other street has a red light, and that the other drivers on that street will respect it, even though we cannot see it ourselves. We risk our lives daily on believing without ever giving it a second thought. Have you ever flown on an airplane on a dark night? Now that is real "blind faith" and believing for sure. Just try flying over the Rockies or over the ocean at night and not "believing".

So why would anyone want to take a chance on eternity simply because they cannot believe? That is the logic of the message we share; "Don't take the chance, just believe in Him". What do you have to lose anyway?

I was having a "chat" on facebook with a couple of young atheists one day, and they asked me this question about my belief in God and eternity; "But what if you are wrong?" And I answered by simply saying, "I have had a wonderful life anyway so I have lost nothing" I then asked a similar question to theirs right back at them. So I simply asked them; "But what if I am right and you are wrong? What have you lost?" I did not get an answer to my question back from them. I hope they are still seriously thinking about that one.

Therefore the basic message of the church in missions is actually simply to "believe in Him" in order to experience the miraculous transformation that such a simple, basic act can and certainly will produce. That is certainly a very secure place to entrust our "believing".

To believe in Him is so much easier than believing in something manmade and capable of failing. It is asking the world to simply believe in the Creator of all things, and He certainly should be considered a reliable target in which to place full trust.

What a joy to go to the world with that message. The answer is quite simple. If you need peace in your life here and a hope for eternity, you simply need to believe in Him. He is the source of both peace for here, and also security on an eternal basis. That simple message certainly works today, and has been working over the centuries as well, so the church can have the confidence to share the message today without any fear whatsoever that it will not perform at present even as it was promised it would do so long ago.

So we go to tell them to simply believe in Him, and that nothing more is required. That is the message of world missions which the church carries with great assurance and confidence into the world today.

Number Eight   *"Should Not Perish"*

THE SECURITY OFFERED BY WORLD MISSIONS

The message of missions is certainly not a negative, nor is it a threat being presented to the hearers in any way whatsoever either. In fact it is just the opposite. It is first of all a guarantee of total protection from any possible negatives for anytime in the future based upon anything we may have done or even "inherited" from our first parents in Eden.

Interestingly it is stated as a wonderful positive but is here actually written using a negative word to express that positive idea; "should NOT perish", and we certainly emphasize the "not" stated here as we go to the world with the message of Calvary, and of God's love so dramatically demonstrated there. The message is not about perishing for sure. Instead it is about "not" perishing, if they simply choose to accept the option of believing in Him, and getting that promised protection personally themselves by doing just that.

That is the protection our message takes to the whole world in our missions outreach. It is not saying, "You are all going to perish!" Instead, it is offering protection from the natural consequence of the world's rebellion and sin by saying, "there is only one solution that is capable of providing protection for anyone, and it is certainly for you as well; simply believe on Jesus!"

Perishing is what we all deserve, but there is another alternative that basically has inserted a, "no way I will let this happen to you if you believe in Me" alternative before the word perish and it is signed by God Himself, and I really trust that signature. For God certainly does not want anyone to perish.

Does anyone remember the line from the old hymn, "Jesus signed my pardon this I surely know; took my place on Calvary so I don't have to go"? That is the positive message we have to present to the world for what would otherwise be an extremely negative alternative of actually perishing eternally.

God tells the church to go tell the world that they need not perish, because He loves them so much He went to the furthest extreme possible to ensure that nobody ever needs to actually have to perish. There is an easy escape route available to everyone, and all anyone needs to do is run to it. It is an easy "exit" from the consequences of sin, and that is our message as we go to our world.

The church's world missions task therefore is to erect more and more "EXIT" signs around our society, as well as around our world to make the alternative to perishing very visible. His sacrifice, and our accepting and believing in it, is the escape route, both from "perishing" but it is also excitedly our entrance into "everlasting life" as well.

So our message and instructions from God relating to world missions is first of all for us to let the world know that such a provision has been made for their protection from having to join Satan for eternity in the place that originally was only intended solely for him and his fallen angels. Therefore the message is simple. Although hell is certainly real, none of Adam's race need end up there. They just need to run as fast as possible to that exit sign to ensure they do not do so.

Secondly, He tells us to simply point the world towards that failure-proof escape route, and lead them away from the eternal destiny to which we were all originally assigned because of sin. It is certainly an exciting message we have for the world, and that is what makes missions so exciting for us as well.

Our fallen race can certainly escape all of the negatives we most surely deserve, but our message to the world is far more than an escape "from" these negatives as terrifying as they may be. Actually our message to the world is primarily one that instead presents an extremely positive and secure escape "to" eternal bliss, and that is certainly what the church's message in world missions is all about. The escape "from" is terrible, but the escape "to" we share with the world is exciting beyond description.

Number Nine   "But Have Everlasting Life"

THE ETERNAL OUTCOME OF WORLD MISSIONS

What an exciting reality! Every successful contact we have with a lost world that produces even just one more positive result gives someone else "everlasting life". Heaven forever; and that is exactly what "eternal life" will mean for everyone we reach with the gospel message in missions, if they then choose to believe and accept the sole solution, which is in Him and Him alone.

But everlasting life is so much more than simply living forever. Living forever could be an eternal life of misery. But that is not the case here for certain. It is an eternal life of bliss beyond our present capacity to even grasp or understand. It is life abundantly that we are offering to the world with God's total authorization for us to do so. It is a "Welcome Home" from God with all of heaven's resources and benefits forever at their disposal, and we have been given the privilege to present it to the world.

No wonder we go so willing into our world with this message and are willing to personally pay such prices to make it possible. It is the number one priority with God, should also be number one priority with the church, and is certainly number one priority for a lost world even if they do not even know that fact as yet. Absolutely nothing is of any higher priority.

Imagine going to a street kid who has absolutely nothing, and is actually at the point of perishing from hunger and cold, and standing before the child there in its desperate condition and saying, "I have been told to tell you that you have just inherited a massive mansion and millions of dollars to go with it as well". What excitement for the child and what a joy even for the message conveyor as well, when that child finds out your message you brought to him is actually true. There would be lots of "jumping for joy" there for certain, but not only by the kid. The bearer of that great news would likely do a "little" jumping as well! I am sure you get the picture!

I would sure love to be there to see his face when he actually realizes your message to him is actually real. And what a wonderful, radical change in reality it would be for him as well. But for us to actually be able to tell the world they have been adopted into the King's family with a home awaiting them in heaven; now there is an exciting story to tell to our world for certain.

Yet "on the other side of the coin" as they say, the tragic consequences of not taking the message to the world is the total negating of all of the provisions of Calvary, because it can work no eternal destiny change miracle for anyone who has never heard.

The Scripture asks clearly, "How can they believe in One of whom they have not heard?" Then it adds, "And how shall they go except they be sent?" It should not be to difficult for us to clearly see missions involved there in that process for certain. Unless we share the message, that child will die on the street without knowing he was actually now a potential "millionaire"!

So this is missions; going, giving, sending and praying for the application of Calvary's sacrifice to become a personal reality to as many around our world as it is possible to have included. It is doing what it is going to take to reach them, to show them God's love, and thereby bring them safely home to Him to revel fully in the glory of His provision of love.

That is the challenge that the church has been presented with today as the task gets continuously larger, and the available time to get this job done gets shorter on a daily basis.

God so loved the world that He gave, and we also quite willingly and even excitedly also give ourselves on the altar of sacrifice to go to our world with the message of His love as well, basically because we so love the God we serve, and we also so love the same world He loves. What exciting possibilities there await us, and also the world to which we go, when we share that combined love from God and from ourselves as well with the world.

I am concluding this world missions section with a personal poem, written when I was about nineteen years of age, in response to the sensing of God's calling on my life at that particular time. And I have never since turned away from that calling!

My Calling

Tonight I looked across the sea
And in vision saw outstretched to me
Hands of people, weeping, crying
"No one has told us, now we're dying
What can wash us white as snow,
Who can save us; do you know?"

People there in deep distress;
People searching for sweet rest,
Dying bound by sin and shame,
Knowing not the Savior came;
Took their sins upon Calvary,
And gave to all salvation free.

Then I heard the Savior say
"Can I count on you today?
Will you go and will you toil
Give your life on foreign soil
Count all other thing but lost
That you might win them to the cross?"

There I stood with head bowed low,
Saw all my plans and ambitions go,
Saw wealth and fame and comforts flee,
Heard naught but Christ on Calvary:

"See what I've done, I died alone
A cross became my royal throne."

Into my heart a burden crept.
I could not pray, I only wept
Oh yes, oh yes, I'll go, I'll go;
My privilege the way to show
To people who in sin and shame
Have never heard the Savior's name.

Scott Hunter

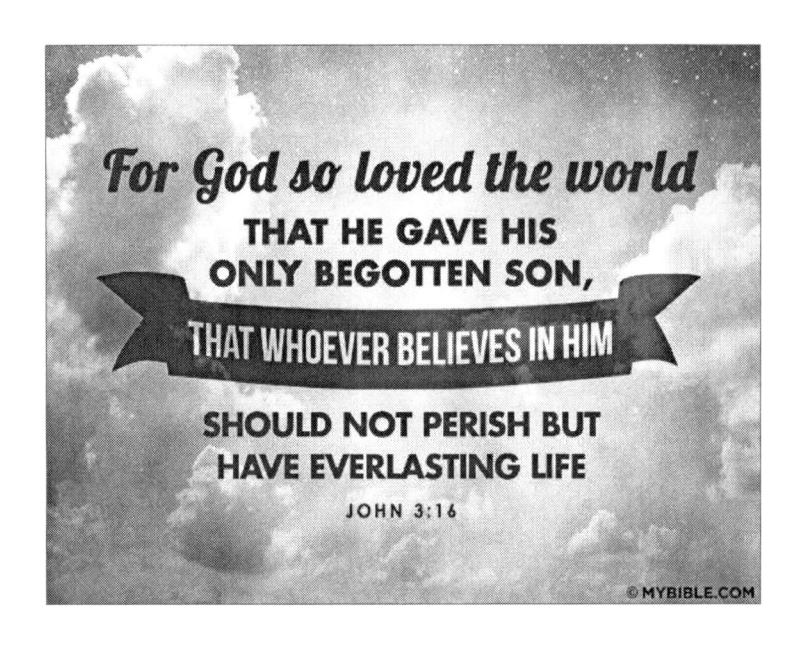

> For God so loved the world **THAT HE GAVE HIS ONLY BEGOTTEN SON, THAT WHOEVER BELIEVES IN HIM** SHOULD NOT PERISH BUT HAVE EVERLASTING LIFE
>
> JOHN 3:16

About the Author

Born in Newfoundland, Canada, December 25, 1943. Graduated from Eastern Pentecostal Bible College in April, 1968; then drove all night from Toronto, Ontario to Cumberland, Maryland and married Nancy Lowery there that same day!

We pastored in Canada until 1972, when we accepted our first appointment as missionaries to Zambia with the Pentecostal Assemblies of Canada. Spent forty years total in world missions to Zambia, South Africa and Malawi, which also included over twenty years in Canada as a full-time missions promoter for the PAOC world missions program.

Worked as the PAOC Field Director of both Zambia and also Malawi at different times

Had a son and a daughter, both born in Zambia. Our son later died suddenly at age 15 of a massive heart attack while going in through the church door. Our daughter lives near us today in the Ottawa, Ontario region!

I am now retired, after returning to Canada from Malawi for open heart surgery with the main artery in my heart one hundred percent block, yet despite that situation having had no sign of any heart attack. The doctor here pointed his finger in the air and said to me, "There must be Someone up there taking care of you!"

I still have a great passion for God and for the world He so loves! I love to write, and am now beginning to feel this is God's new leading for me since my heart condition prevents long-term overseas commitments at this time. Love to speak on missions and have spoken in hundreds of churches in Canada and also overseas.

I have raised many hundreds of thousands of dollars for missions without usually even asking for money. Instead people have simply responded to the challenge presented, and then given freely or often ask me how they can become involved personally in world missions both personally and also financially.

Scott Hunter snhunter@gmail.com

Scott and Nancy Hunter

CPSIA information can be obtained at www.ICGtesting.com
Printed in the USA
BVOW030416220513

321329BV00007B/33/P